it, and this day the Dominion of Canada is proclaimed; and, as Canadians, no longer confined within petty Provincial limits, but members of a larger nationality, New Brunswick and Nova Scotia, Quebec and Ontario, join hands, and a shout of rejoicing goes up from the four millions of people who are now linked together for weal or for woe, to work out in common the destinies of a united British America.

The prelimi... Union of the B... contemplated a... Canadas and... vinces, with pr...n... at some futu... of Red River, and British C... of this project complishment only a matte... Island has to remain Newfoundlan... throw in h... Provinces. B... concerned, th... the whole of... title of the D... *accompli.* Th... Confederacy o... mere matter... the occasion... Council, the... done all that... legislation. A... Newfoundland and Prince Edward Island, the whole machinery for their admission has already been provided. So soon as they are prepared to enter the Confederacy, all they have to do is to express through their Legislatures a desire to that effect, and by an Order in Council, with the consent of the Dominional Parliament without any further reference to the Imperial Parliament, Her Majesty will admit them. In like manner, as regards the Red River Settlement and the North West Territory, so soon as the Senate and House of Commons of Canada are in a position to organize Governments for these regions, they have only to intimate their wishes, and Her Majesty will give effect to them. In its most important aspects, therefore, we may look upon the Confederation of the whole of British North America as completed. The incorporation of Rupert's Land and the North

West Territory is made... act of... to cast a libellous impu... fitness for the high career... now entering. And as reg... Provinces, which have stil... ernments of their own, we... sume that, studying what... own weal, as well as looki... ral advantage, both from a... a Colonial point of view,... Confedera... they will...edily... give... which e... over the... ers to... whole of Her Majes-... out British North

...to-day an event of... tance than the Con-... ...three or four Pro-... two of the Maritime ...anada. We celebrate ...a new nationality; to ...the interests of ...lization over a terri-... of the ancient Ro-... too, than the terri-...olled by the great ...ic, and with a popu-...hat with which the ... their career ninety ...duties, therefore, of ...he hopes and aspira-...future, there is room ...ough for the purest ...ftiest ambition. Let ...Canadians—using the word in its new and large acceptation—will worthily fulfil the duties which Providence has confided to them.

From the commencement of the movement until its auspicious consummation to-day, THE GLOBE has been ever its zealous and persevering advocate. We have striven to meet objections, to remove obstacles, to smooth down asperities. We have endeavoured to combat

This editorial from

The Globe

of July 1, 1867, was written by George Brown, founder, owner, and editor.

THE NATION MAKERS

1867 | 1967

Published on the occasion of the Centennial of Canadian Confederation. The preparation of the manuscript was subsidized by the Centennial Commission.

Ouvrage publié à l'occasion du Centenaire de la Confédération Canadienne redigé grâce à une subvention de la Commission du Centenaire.

Books by JOSEPH SCHULL

LAURIER
Great Stories of Canada
THE SALT-WATER MEN
BATTLE FOR THE ROCK
SHIPS OF THE GREAT DAYS

JOSEPH SCHULL

The Nation Makers

Illustrations by

IRMA COUCILL

Macmillan 1967 Toronto

Printed in Canada for the Macmillan Company of Canada Limited, 70 Bond Street, Toronto, by the T. H. Best Printing Company Limited.

For

MICHAEL JOHN ANTHONY

Author's Note

THIS SMALL BOOK is an attempt to distil the essence of a very large and complicated story. I would hope that it might convey to the general reader some sense of the characters of the men involved and of the dimensions of their work. I would also hope, in this Centennial Year, that it might stimulate some to seek a wider and more intimate knowledge of the nation's past. They would find much, as I have, in the following books, which have been my principal sources: *John A. Macdonald – The Young Politician* and *John A. Macdonald – The Old Chieftain* by Donald Creighton (Toronto: Macmillan, 1952 and 1955); *The Road to Confederation* by Donald Creighton (Toronto: Macmillan, 1964); *Brown of The Globe* (two volumes) by J. M. S. Careless (Toronto: Macmillan, 1959 and 1963); *The Life and Times of Confederation* by P. B. Waite (Toronto: University of Toronto Press, 1965); *Sir George Etienne Cartier* by John Boyd (Toronto: Macmillan, 1927); and *Sir Alexander Tilloch Galt* by Oscar Douglas Skelton (Toronto: McClelland and Stewart, 1966).

Contents

Illustrations

1

British North America

No ONE HAD DECIDED, no one even knew it, but 1864 had become the year of decision. It was 372 years since the coming of Columbus. It was 367 years since the first footfall of an Englishman on a North American shore. It was 330 years since Jacques Cartier, crossing the sea-tracks of the Portuguese, had carried the banner of France into the Gulf of St. Lawrence. Now, after the wars and wanderings of three tumultuous centuries, Spanish and Portuguese were a fading memory. The Indian tribes who had seen the white man come were dwindling remnants going the way of the past. The way of the future lay with the English and French.

Each was a people that had dreamed of empire, and had seen the wreck of the dream. Wolfe on the Plains of Abraham had put an end to New France, bequeathed the continent to England. Yet within a generation rebellious, victorious Englishmen in the War of the Revolution had wrenched the half of it

1

away. The thirteen richest colonies had become the United States of America, never again to know an English king. The lands of the king were left as a northern fringe, scattered, diverse, and shared by a subject people.

Newfoundland, flung out to the Atlantic from the continent's eastern shore, seemed hardly a part of the western world at all. It was first of the English landfalls, oldest of English colonies. It sprawled, a glowering sentinel, in the wide St. Lawrence gateway walled by the Labrador cliffs. Yet its back was turned to the mainland waste it guarded; its people looked to the sea, lived by the sea. They were sons of men who had come for fish, not land. They moved in waters hoary with old wars, always for England, and for land and fish. But only England and the fish concerned them. The new world guardian was an old-world outpost.

Southward across the Gulf, Prince Edward Island sheltered in warmer water. It had been French once but the French were gone, banished in ancient wars. Seamen had come here who no longer sailed. Fishermen's sons had given up their trade. Forests had been cleared away, the timber spent; islanders built no more ships. Now, English, Irish, Scots, they tilled the land, a fruitful land long known and deeply loved. It fed its people well, this sea-ringed garden, and closed their horizons within its narrow shores. Islanders lived with plenty and lived to themselves. They wanted little that the mainland offered, and offered less than little in return.

Around the island curved a long, harsh coast,
shared by two mainland colonies. To seaward lay
Nova Scotia, rich and proud, settled and old. It had
known the wars and seen the uprooting of peoples,
the agonies and hopes of change and turmoil. That
was behind it now. Hardly a memory of the French
remained, those first Acadians driven out by conquest. The Revolution's anguish was forgotten. Thousands of British, loyal to their king, had streamed back
homeless from the rebel colonies. They had found
new homes and built their lives anew. They had bred
up sons more British than before. There was wealth
in farms and forests, mines and fish, wealth above all
in ships. Each spring the creeks and bays fed down
the hulls, the masts were stepped, new canvas bil-
lowed out. The Bluenose sailors were known on every
sea. The merchant princes traded with the world,
profited from all the world. The St. Lawrence gloomed
at their backs amid its forests, key to a mainland that
was hardly thought of. Fifty ships went to the seas
from Nova Scotia for every ship that climbed the
inland river. A thousand miles of coastline gave on
water. A single narrow link of fourteen miles moored
the near-island to the land above. The colony strained
on the map like a ship at anchor, reaching away to
England and the world. And heart and interest
pointed the way of the map.

New Brunswick was a newer Nova Scotia, peopled
by kindred strains, served by the oceans too. New
Brunswick ships sailed with the Bluenose ships, New
Brunswick timber built them. Eastward and south

salt water washed the shores, drawing men outward to the seamen's trades. But west and north a lovely valley ran, carved by the swift St. John through inland forest. Men followed it against the water's flow, felling the timber, sending it down to the sea, hacking out farmlands when the stumps were burned. Life broadened north along the river's length, a different life, a life of mainland men, yet still unlinked with other mainland men.

Beyond the forests at the valley's head the St. Lawrence climbed from the sea, leading to Canada. Where rivers ran men followed, life began. Homes rose, wealth grew, and there was wealth above. There was limitless promise always beckoning west. Yet there was wealth here too, close to the sea. Timber and fish and salt were good, known smells; old callings called the loudest. Canadians were still far off and little known. New Brunswickers looked east.

Canadians beyond their forests looked to themselves. Here lay, threaded along an endless chain of water, the heart of the oldest battleground, the homeland of two peoples. Once French, it now was British. Yet a million British subjects were wholly French. They lived out lives drawn from an alien root, yet no root struck more deeply in this soil. None held more firmly. Conquest had severed Frenchmen from old France. It had only bound them closer to this land, treasuring more dearly what the land had given, the homes and laws, the faith and tongue that joined them. They had not changed under an English king. They had not been won by the cries of revolution.

Conquered, accepting conquest, still unchanged, the Frenchman had repulsed the American dream. He had not resigned his own. He was French, Canadian, British, and himself.

Around him was the thrust of newer men. They had come, the conquerors, when conquest came. They had flooded in from the south, an angry tide, when rebel brothers wrecked the imperial dream. Conquerors no more, they would not be Americans. Britannia in the north should rise again, giving back homes and hopes that had been lost, fashioning a new land of the old land's fibre. They and their sons and thousands of their kin had cleared and built and wrought through the years since. They had suffered and endured, quarrelled and succeeded. Widening and always west their work went on. Bustling, impatient, Protestant, and proud – British in name, American in their ways – they longed to hew and tame and shape a nation, always in the British image that they knew. Always the other British barred their way – American in nothing, Catholic in all – the British subjects who spoke and thought in French.

Canada. It climbed along the St. Lawrence, rich and settled. It groped through western wilderness to the shores of the Great Lakes. Each year new thousands hacked the forests down. The farmlands broadened and the roads reached out. There were towns and cities and the smoke of railways. Yet men divided found no way together, no tie with the other British east and west. The imperial river linked them with the ocean. The mighty inland reaches tugged at their thoughts. Still there was no shared hope with men by the sea. Only the moccasin and the great canoe took to the trails and rivers beyond the lakes.

There rock and forest rolled away to prairie, a blankness on a map, an empty sea, dotted with island clusters of lonely men. This was the great North-west, the Territories, vague in allegiance as it was in name. The British flag flew here where any flew, but Indians and buffalo-hunters roamed beneath it, seekers of furs and squatters on new lands. They were too far, too few, too strange, to men of the east. Who in the east could know their ways or hopes?

Still there were men beyond them more remote. Where prairie ended mountains towered up, walling away the east and its concerns, sloping to another sea. Here British Columbia fronted on the Pacific. An island swam beside it, British too, bearing Vancouver's name. He was a seaman who had come by sea, the western way, as almost all men here. Only the rivers had pierced the mountain wall, and only the men who had followed them for furs. The new men come from the west were here for gold. They were here for timber and for fish and land. With mountains at their backs they looked to the sea, westward and south. The link with the east was a half-forgotten thread, twisting in white-lashed foam through roaring gorges, old as the timbers of the old *bateaux* rotting in mountain whirlpools.

These were the colonies under the Union Jack. So they lay in that year of destiny, 1864. They had given prosperous lives to many men. They had sheltered behind the shield of British power. They had learned to govern themselves in the British way, and had taught the mother that they meant to do it. Yet they were still a fringe of scattered peoples, of regions coveted by a greater nation. They hovered at the edge of a mighty conflict, threatened by changes that no man could measure. They had feared the United States as a peaceful giant; she was doubly dangerous, torn by civil war. They would lie beside her when that struggle ended, sons of a distant mother whose power was waning. What if the wounded giant turned to the north?

This was the fear, and there was more than fear. The colonies were homes of thriving men. They could not remain forever as they were. They were men who lived in history willy-nilly, drawing from its fountains, swept on in its stream. They yearned for something more than what they had. They felt the imminence of change and choice. A hope, a promise, and a discontent hovered over all and filled the northern air. Parted by distance and by wilderness, parted by interest and by warring bloods, they groped in common for a sense of greatness. And greatness was not far off; the men were stirring.

2

Time Ripened

THE WHITE-BRICK Legislative Building stood on the heights of Quebec, looking out over the wide sweep of the St. Lawrence. It was the home of the parliament of Canada. Not far from here Jacques Cartier had once stood, the first man of the old world to set foot on this rock. Champlain had followed him to found the city. From here New France had grown and here, on that grey September morning when the red-coats climbed the cliff, New France had passed away. Yet only a name, a dream of kings had passed; a people remained. In this white building looking from the heights two peoples mingled and contended still.

The session of 1864 was now in progress. For several weeks the sixty-five members for Upper Canada and the sixty-five members for Lower Canada had met and debated together, all of them oppressed by a common sense of futility. On this morning of May 20 the thickly-carpeted oval chamber with its ornate galleries looking down on rows of walnut desks

8

stood silent and empty. Its doors would open as usual at mid afternoon, but the members would come together only to quarrel aridly and accomplish nothing. Government was on the brink of another crisis, another deadlock.

In a smaller committee chamber somewhere along the corridors heavy-leaded windows stood open to the spring air. Sixteen men had filed into the room, some alone, some in murmuring groups of two or three. A seventeenth had been standing at the head of a long table, waiting for them. He was tall, raw-boned, red-haired, quite obviously alight with purpose and as obviously prepared for trouble. He strode to the door as the last man took his seat, turned the key in the lock and put the key in his pocket. 'Now, gentlemen,' said George Brown, 'you must talk about this matter as you cannot leave this room without coming to me.'

No man rose to protest, though there were half a dozen at least who had no wish to be here. They were delegates of all the parties represented in that other chamber. Brown's enemies and Brown's friends, and some who were wary neutrals. It was Brown who had brought them here but it was not Brown who caged them; it was the old dilemma of government. They were all a part of it, they were all trapped by it.

As politicians, they wore the sober labels that distinguished varying views of common affairs. They were Liberals or Conservatives, they were Rouges or Bleus. They fought elections, they formed governments, they debated on the country's business, always as representatives of a single united people. The French Bleu was the formal counterpart of the English Conservative, the French Rouge of the English Liberal; and so alliances were formed, so debate went on. Yet debate had become meaningless, for every alliance was fiction. The party labels meant nothing, for each party was divided. Government was coming to a standstill, for no group could govern. Beneath the formal differences and belying the formal unities was the older, uglier rift.

This Canada, one in name, was two in fact. Neither the old wars, nor the rebellion of twenty-seven years ago, nor the union that followed rebellion had brought the peoples together. Lower Canada remained the homeland of the French. Upper Canada remained the province of the English, steadily outstripping the French and determined on its own way. This union, these forms of responsible government, had all been made by the English to promote a single nation. They had all failed. The two provinces could not be ruled as one. These men knew it. They had tried their hands at it, most of them, balancing between the claims of French and English, bargaining and bribing for votes. Some of them were still trying, scarred and soiled and disheartened, while paralysis came on.

Hovering over them all, dominant from the beginning, was the settled conviction of conquerors that Frenchmen must become English. It lay at the heart of their troubles and had made most of them. It had led to the framing of the union, to this parliament of which they were all a part, and now to this threat of chaos and collapse. They had come together today, whether they knew it or not, to revise that conviction.

George Brown would not have said so, not yet. He was here with another purpose that seemed wholly different. His cry was 'Representation by Population – Justice for Upper Canada' – that justice which would recognize the first principle of parliamentary government by giving a majority of members to a greater population. There were now in the whole of Canada a million and a half English. There were only a million French. Yet in that parliament of the union, with its two sections balanced, French and English were equal. Five hundred thousand citizens, denied their rightful influence, could not be denied much longer. Brown was the proof of that, standing at the head of this table. The meeting itself was proof. Brown had forced it onto reluctant men because he moved with the weight of the times.

He was a Protestant and a Scot. He had come to Toronto in 1843, a man in his middle twenties. It was six years, then, since the French had been crushed in rebellion, and only two since union of the Canadas. Brown had leaped to the support of Upper Canada's causes; he had grown rich. He was founder and owner of the great Toronto *Globe*, the very voice of the province, rasping and British, powerful and Protestant. By birth, by instinct and the tug of his whole being, he was drawn to oppose the French, and oppose the Church that seemed to rule and teach them. He had come to a country conquered by the

11

British, he had come to a province made by Protestants; he dreamed of the westward march of a mighty
people, always one, Protestant and British. He had
watched his Upper Canada forging ahead, in growth,
in progress, promise and population. He saw the
priest-led people along the St. Lawrence only as the
burden of conquest, the weight that dragged, the
barrier to be trampled down. Or so he had seemed to
see them for long years. For long years, detested and
feared by the French, he had been the prophet and
bigot, trumpeting the will of a growing English
majority.

Facing him at this table sat George Etienne Cartier,
leader of the Catholic French of Lower Canada. He
was not leader of them all; he was a Bleu with Rouge
enemies as bitter as the Conservative enemies who
fought the Liberal, Brown. But he was still the most
powerful man in Lower Canada. Around Cartier the
battle of peoples had raged for years, and around him
still the great decision must turn. He knew it and
enjoyed it; he was small enough for that. Yet, if he
loved power, he had purpose too. He felt the weight
he carried.

He was short and bristling, prematurely grey, alive
with reckless vitality. The high, thin voice was often
raised in song, oftener still in floods of jangling speech.
His English, said his enemies in parliament, had the
sound of someone 'shaking a bag of nails', yet out of
the bag came facts as hard as nails. When he answered
Brown he spoke for all the French, enemies and
friends alike. He would not yield to this 'justice'

Brown proclaimed. He remembered an older time that Brown forgot.

He was only fifty as he sat here now. But his thoughts went back from this council room to a cold November morning twenty-seven years before. He would never forget the smoke of Saint-Dénis, the flame-gashed smother of battle, the spatter and sing of bullets, and the blur of dull-red coats. He had been Cartier the rebel then, the maker of rebel songs, the hater of English rule. Then he had been Cartier the fugitive, the man with a price on his head, stumbling through snowy woods for the American border. None of it had lasted long, neither the fear nor the flight nor the hatred. He had come home to be pardoned by the English, to become the student again, to turn to the law and rise in politics. But he had also come home to see this union made.

He remembered Lord Durham on his tall white horse, the princely pacifier who had come from England, riding with his retinue through sullen streets. He was to bring peace, he was to bring justice to both the restless Canadas. And what had come out of it all? This union. This single Canada, still with its two sections. This rigged parliament. A false and forced equality that denied the rule of numbers, because the mutinous French were then a majority. Locked in a single state, steadily overborne, Frenchness must yield itself to English ways. That was Lord Durham's hope. What bayonets had not done, policy and time would do.

Policy and time had gone another way. The Upper

13

Canadians now outnumbered the French; the minority had become the majority. But this Canada was still governed by the parliament the English had made; its two sections were still equal. Sixty-five members here answered to sixty-five. The paper bulwarks stood, sheltering the French now. Yet for how long? How long could growth and power be denied? Cartier had no answer.

Nor had he any wish to stand forever, stock-still, behind the crumbling walls of the past. Cartier could dream his dreams as well as Brown. He feared the Americans as much, he hoped as much for this country. He had had a hand in its making, he had grown and prospered here. He had known the taste of power, the thirst for greatness. Yet whose greatness? What did it call for, what must be given up? This man before him had attacked the schools of the French. He had attacked their Church, their tongue, their laws and customs. In this single province, when the will of the majority prevailed, it must be the will of the English, the will of George Brown. Greatness might come, but only English greatness, the slow extinction of French and Catholic life, the lingering death of a people.

Near Cartier sat the lean, graceful, long-nosed lawyer of Upper Canada, John A. Macdonald. He was a man not yet unfolded, though few men knew it here, least of all himself. To many around this table he seemed to be too well known, as the deft manipulator of men, the hard drinker and the boon companion, the smiling hatcher of political plots. Through twenty

SIR GEORGE ETIENNE CARTIER

years in parliament he had dealt with things as they were, mastering the ways of the game, trading for place and power. Through fourteen years he had lived with an ailing wife, watching at sick-beds, nursing hopeless hope. Now power was fading and the wife was gone. The boon companion's smile masked lonely depths. The politician saw the end of the game.

As leader of English Conservatives, he might have seemed the natural ally of Brown and the other English. Instead, he stood with Cartier at the head of the union's government. To Brown he had seemed for years the tool of the French – clever, corrupt, and malleable, thinking only of power. To himself and those who followed him he had been the practical man, working out progress in peace. There were other things than schools and tongues and churches. There were other hopes for the peoples of this land. Let them ripen awhile, let tongues and churches be. Let people remain as they were, working and growing together; that had been Macdonald's thought. Steadily, skilfully, deviously, detesting Brown in all things, he had fought Brown's central cause. He would not support that Upper Canadian 'justice', that Representation by Population that would make the English supreme. He was not prepared to crush the will of the French; that way had always failed. Time, he had thought, might bring its own solution if government could carry on. Yet government was coming to a standstill and Macdonald was here at bay, forced here by Brown. Time was running out and he saw no solution in sight.

Alexander Galt had proposed a solution seven years

before. He was of this committee too – portly, hand-some, and rich, a landholder and railway-builder whose dreams transcended money. They transcended the quarrels of race, religion, and tongue. These divided the Canadas. What joined them? There was common allegiance to the British Crown. There was the common hope of prospering on the mighty con-tinent. If government strained the allegiance and blocked the hope, why should not government be changed?

This 'legislative' union that now joined the Canadas was a system of central government in which one parliament made all the laws for both peoples. It was unworkable because it tried to force them both into a common mould, to make them alike in every detail of their lives. French legislators would not be ruled by English in the things nearest their hearts; nor would English be ruled by French. They differed in religion and on the matter of schools; they quarrelled over prized traditions and cherished privileges. They fought each other and blocked each other because they were determined to remain themselves, to hold to the things they loved. Yet what were all those differences to the great things held in common? They shared this land and their hopes lay here together.

There was another government that had grown beside them, but grown on a different plan. The United States were joined by a 'federal' union, in which each state was a sovereignty to itself. The state made laws and spoke for education, it controlled and shaped the daily lives of its people. Only on great

17

affairs of common concern did it tender allegiance to the central government. Yet the common concerns had bound the states together. This union of free-willed peoples had held for eighty years and had grown to be a mighty nation. Why should not such a plan be the answer for Canada?

Galt had proposed that the old union be dissolved, and that the provinces come together again in a new Federal union. Each would be sovereign in its separate concerns, yet repose its common concerns in a central government. Side by side, with the Crown as their great link, the two peoples might then shape lives of their own. Free of each other where they chose to be free, they would freely join for the work they wished to share. This would be a stronger union than before. It would lift the stifling cloud of the old fears, it would open the way ahead to new horizons. Why should it be confined by the borders of Canada? Why should it not reach down the St. Lawrence to the sea, outward in time, to embrace the great west? The men by the sea were different from Canadians, the men of the west were different again. Here in this plan was promise for them all; freedom, diversity, a common will. The facts of population would prevail; this would be a British nation. Yet within it would remain the French, secure at last in every dear concern, partners in freedom and in purpose too.

The plan was older than Galt, but Galt had given it life. It was slowly taking a grip on the minds of men. Yet it meant that Brown must abandon many hopes. It called for a trust that Cartier would not give. It meant for Macdonald the American way, and what had that come to now? He saw the mighty nation torn apart, the clash of states bent on their separate wills. He saw the blood and agony of civil war. He would not have that for Canada; he would not have federal union. In this at least they had all been as one, Brown, Cartier, and himself. Most of the men at this table, enemies and friends alike, had held apart from the plan. Yet the tide of the times had been stronger than them all. They were here to talk of it now.

There were eight meetings round the table in that committee room in Quebec. Through eight days of talk, jealous, unhopeful, wary, and suspicious men retraced the road from the conquest, bandied old phrases battered by the years. They emerged, it seemed, as empty of hope as ever. The committee, Brown reported to the parliament on June 14, had only decided to consider the question further. Even to that Macdonald had not agreed.

Yet, on that same day, the government in which Cartier and Macdonald were the pillars of power tumbled to its final fall. There was no government to take its place, no man who would even attempt to carry on. Two days later, as the members of the headless parliament were assembling in the oval chamber, they saw a strange sight. John A. Macdonald walked up the carpeted aisle, brushed by some curious watchers making for their seats, and exchanged a few words with Brown. What the old enemies said no one then knew, but Quebec began to buzz with the talk of meetings. Strangely assorted groups of

19

friends and enemies went into hotel rooms, silent, and came out more silent still. It was ten days later that the announcement came in parliament. George Brown, John A. Macdonald, and George Etienne Cartier had entered a coalition and were pledged to the search for a plan of federal union. The barrier of the old conviction had begun to crumble. A new hope was stirring amid the wreckage.

3

The Men by the Sea

BELOW QUEBEC, at the mouth of the long river, there had been other stirrings. Nova Scotia, New Brunswick, Prince Edward Island, and Newfoundland pursued their separate lives. In each there had been a long struggle to win responsible government. Now there was too much government. Each colony had its little legislature and its self-important men, following their own ambitions. They were small ambitions, for the field was small. They were often narrow and oftener still divisive, for no colony would share its concerns with another. Each with its tariffs strangling the other's trade, each with its pride and rivalry and interest, the four little states went on as petty nations.

Their British governors presided over affairs but had lost the power to direct them. The motherland was growing impatient. She had yielded up many freedoms and retained too many burdens. These restless sons were determined to govern themselves but they still had to be defended. They could not live long alone, as scattered scraps of territory by the side of the United States. Yet they still wished to be British and could not be set adrift. They must find their independence and the strength they would need to maintain it in some other course.

Statesmen in London, studying the map, saw four little blots of land, two afloat, two tied to the mainland, all clustered about the entrance to the Gulf of St. Lawrence. It seemed obvious that they should join together. Quite as obviously, in the longer future, the united Maritime provinces should reach up the St. Lawrence to link themselves with Canada. This was the shape of the future, seen from London. It was the plan that British governors urged on the colonies. The age of railways was already at hand. Only united provinces, pooling their resources, could find the money to build them. Only a British union could confront the American union, with at least a hope of enduring, at the end of the Civil War.

Charles Tupper, premier of Nova Scotia, heard all these arguments from British governors. They were familiar enough. Joseph Howe, the great predecessor whom he had just deposed from power, had advanced some of them himself. The old man walked the streets of Halifax now, glowering and bitter, or went off on tiresome voyages as a Fisheries Inspector, the petty post the British government had given him when he retired from politics. But there were few ideas stirring in the air today that Howe had not known first.

Howe had hoped for union and hoped for railways. He had seen railways as the spine of a future nation. He had tried to join the mainland Maritime provinces and to bridge the seven hundred miles of wilderness that divided the sea from Canada. Nor had he stopped there. He had given a thrilling promise years before that many alive would yet hear the whistle of the locomotive in the passes of the Rocky Mountains and travel from the Atlantic to the Pacific in a matter of days. Greatest of the early dreamers, he had stood on the brink of success, with plans for railways made and with men in the Maritimes and in England and the Canadas fired with his own enthusiasm. For one brief moment at the peak of Howe's career the promise of steel-linked union had hovered over the continent. But his plans had collapsed amid haggling and fears and suspicions, before the great distances and the giant obstacles. Space and the wilderness and little men, all had defeated Howe. The Maritime colonies were still petty and divided. The Canadians lived apart beyond their forests.

The motherland still persisted in one of its hopes. It saw in the linking-up of the sea-side peoples at least the beginning of union. But the men in London did not see the difficulties. They were home-grown difficulties, small and parochial, chronic and enduring. What would a union change? Together or apart, four colonies or one, they would still be dependent on England in the face of the United States. They would still be a small community living on its own produce, trading in ships and fish. If separate colonies were joined tariffs would have to be abandoned, trade would be disturbed. If four governments became one, what of the office-holders deprived of office? They were the men who would have to make the union, and many would deprive themselves. Why should they? This was no plan like Howe's. The thought of an inward march across the continent, despite its enormous difficulties appealed to the imagination. It struck fire. There was no fire in this project of Maritime union. Each time a spark had been struck it had smouldered and gone out.

Yet there was the feeling everywhere that some change was near. It troubled the Maritimes as surely as the Canadas; it made easterners look west and westerners look east, disturbed by common doubts. Whatever the outcome of the Civil War, the continent would not be the same. Britain had favoured the states of the Southern Confederacy and incurred the resentment of the North. The North seemed to be winning, and its great armies would lie close along British borders when the war ended. Even if they did not move, even if the United States made no hostile gesture, there would be other forces to deal with. There would be the attractions of the mighty neighbours as well as the fear.

To many in the United States, and to some in the British colonies, it had seemed certain that the future of North America lay under the Stars and Stripes. That vision of 'manifest destiny' had not been lost in the war. It would surely revive with the peace. Thirty million Americans would resume their march to the west, carried by railways now, throwing their steel ahead of them into the wilderness that led to the Pacific. Could the British stand apart? Why should they wish to? They were a million men in the Maritimes, two and a half million in the Canadas, a few scattered thousands in the lands of the far-off west. For all their growth they lived, compared to the Americans, in purposeless stagnation. Hundreds of thousands of them lived on trade with the Americans, for every lane of the continent ran north and south. The Maritime colonies traded with New England, the Canadas traded with the central states, the distant west was hardly divided at all, in spite of flags and borders. The flags still waved, but now for how much longer? Trade was a mighty magnet pulling southward, and only a mightier purpose could resist it.

It stirred unsurely, if it stirred at all, when Charles Tupper rose in the provincial legislature of Nova Scotia on March 28, 1864. He was forty-three years old, a brash, blunt, thrusting bulldog of a man who had fought his way to power and loved the feel of it. As a doctor, he had finished his training in Edinburgh and come home to ride the roads of Cumberland County, day and night, near and far. Now he was a politician, the 'man-midwife', in Howe's bitter phrase. But he had coolly retorted that he would deliver the province of Howe, and he had kept his word. The old man was down though he would never be forgotten, never without influence. Tupper was the new man, and a strong one, but he was already restless within the narrow borders of his province.

RT. HON. SIR CHARLES TUPPER

He had spoken, as everyone spoke from time to time, of that old dream of Howe's, a union of all the British in North America. He had been on hand for the banquetings a year before, when Thomas D'Arcy McGee came down from Canada at the head of a hundred journalists. That poet and politician and newspaperman had had a nice turn of Irish wit, a deft way with Maritimers, a persuasive vision of the mighty nation-to-be. He and his friends had preached it and Tupper had listened and endorsed it, but without much enthusiasm. Union was good to talk of with visitors from beyond the forests, but the forests were still there. They were still unspanned by railways. There had been other talk and plans since that first plan of Howe's, and even a new agreement. Yet everything had collapsed once more in bitterness and recrimination. If those quarrelling, divided Canadas could not keep faith with the Maritimers even on a railway contract, what were the hopes for union?

Nor did he see much hope of uniting the Maritime colonies. British governors might point to many advantages, but Tupper knew the pitfalls. He knew his Nova Scotia and he knew its neighbours. They were restless and fretful and anxious about the Americans, but they were still small in their views. They clung to a fading past and would not be easily changed. They thought as much of their pockets as they thought of nation-building, and it was difficult to show where profit lay in union. Yet it was the business of politicians to be hopeful, to think big and to talk big. Who could tell what might come of it? Bigness and restlessness were a part of Tupper's nature; he wanted 'to have a dash at somebody . . . at least to shiver a lance'. He stood up in the House on that March afternoon, tired of the stagnant air of his little province. He rose to raise a wind and let it blow.

He proposed to the members before him that the old question of a union of the Maritime colonies be once again considered. He suggested that a conference be arranged and that delegates be appointed to attend. He spoke with his usual vigour and his usual ample verbosity on the many virtues of union. Then he sat down, to a stir of polite applause from his own side of the aisle.

Across from him, as the leader of the Liberal opposition, sat Adams George Archibald. He was a cool and elegant lawyer, one of the aristocrats of Nova Scotia, and he had always supported Howe. He had taken Howe's place as the leader of the Liberal Party. He would have to speak for union even though Tupper proposed it, because it was still Howe's plan. Or rather an echo of Howe; it was not a plan at all. Tupper was talking of talk and nothing was likely to come of it, but the man in the shoes of Howe could not oppose him. Archibald agreed that a conference might be desirable.

Beside Archibald the shaggy Jonathan McCully shrugged and grinned. Huge and shambling, limping on a big left foot from which he had lost two toes, McCully had been school teacher, journalist, lawyer, and politician. He was not to be taken in by Charles Tupper. Everyone talked of union and no one acted.

Union was like the weather. Tupper was looking for issues, dispute, debate; something to divide the Liberals. He would not get it. McCully agreed with Archibald that a conference ought to be held, and no one denied it. One long, dull, rambling day concluded discussion. The resolution was passed and the House went on with its business.

Now it was the turn of Samuel Leonard Tilley, premier of New Brunswick. He had heard the arguments of British governors too. He was small and quiet-spoken where Tupper was loud. The ways of the one-time druggist still persisted; he was soothing, solicitous, a careful listener. Yet nothing he heard had given much hope for a union, great or small. The railway plans with the Canadas had collapsed; that project was dead. He was close to Nova Scotia but he was closer still to Maine, with the long eastern shoulder of the state crowding his western border. When Americans talked of railways they usually built them, and there was talk now of a 'Western Extension' line that would link Saint John with Portland. It would only be talk till the end of the Civil War, but what then? If New Brunswick trade were fed into the great Atlantic port on the Maine coast its loyalties would soon follow. There would be no more thought of Canada, little of Nova Scotia, and even less of the motherland. The strength of the British connection would wither away.

It did not seem likely that a conference on Maritime union would do much to dispel that fear. Yet Tupper had advanced the idea, the British Governor of New

Brunswick was enthusiastic about it, and talk was at least cheap. Sometimes it was even helpful. On April 9 Tilley proposed that New Brunswick attend the meeting. His House agreed, and agreed to appoint delegates.

Prince Edward Island watched the doings on the mainland from across Northumberland Strait. It had gone its own way always and it still intended to do so. It had no public debts, while the other provinces had many. There were no railways and there was no thought of them. Boats could cross the Strait in the open seasons, and it was no hardship in winter to be shut away by ice. Life was apart and free of mainland meddling. The wars of politics were private wars, always revolving round a central problem.

The Island's comfortable farmers did not own their lands. They held them as the tenants of English proprietors who had received their grants from the king, almost a century before. It was a creaking remnant of feudalism, bitterly resented in the new world. Most of the proprietors had never seen the island, few did much for their properties, but all were persistent and firm in collecting their rents. They could only be got rid of by being bought out, and there had never been money for that on Prince Edward Island. Could the money be found on the mainland, in this scheme for Maritime union, this talk of pooling resources?

John Hamilton Gray did not think so. He was Premier now, a bearded cavalry colonel who had retired from the British army to come home to island politics. George Coles, the grizzled Charlottetown brewer who had once been in Gray's place, was equally sceptical. So was Edward Palmer, the craggy, cranky lawyer. Each had fought Gray and was likely to fight him again, but they all agreed in this. W. H. Pope, the handsome Provincial Secretary, was a younger man and a dreamer and A. A. Macdonald was the youngest of them all, in his middle thirties and just on the edge of politics. These two had hopes but the others had only suspicions. They saw no money in the talk of maritime union. The talk of pooling resources meant also the pooling of debts, mainland debts. Yet the young men were eager, and it was dangerous to thrust them aside. Talk itself was dangerous when it smelled of mainland scheming. Islanders should be on hand to watch their interests. Or so it seemed to the Premier, beset by old and young. Gray agreed to the conference and agreed to appoint his watchers.

By the end of April the three colonies were committed to a meeting and to the appointment of delegates. Newfoundland had not been thought of, and was not interested. Even in the three the interest quickly waned. Through a late spring and on into early summer the plan slept. Fishermen went to sea, farmers were out on the land. The ships came and went in the crowded ports and politicians were busy on other affairs. Rumours came of the tumbling of governments in Canada, the passing of resolutions and the making of coalitions, but they seemed as remote as ever. The French and English were at their quarrelling still. They were still blamed for the collapse of the railway plans. Bankrupt one day, building and bragging the next, they were men not to be trusted. Maritimers had no interest in talk of Canadian union and less in talk of their own. The wind that Tupper had hoped for had not risen. No province had yet named delegates for the conference, no date had been set, and no place.

Then, on July 9 came a startling letter from Canada. It was written by Lord Monck, Governor General of the province, to Sir Richard Graves MacDonnell, Governor of Nova Scotia. It informed him of the coalition that had come together to frame a plan for the federation of the colonies. It requested on behalf of the Canadians that they might be allowed to attend the conference on Maritime union.

Coming from a sister colony, the request could hardly be refused. Neither could it be acquiesced in unless a conference were held. The inconvenient Canadians had brought the plan to life. Those April resolutions would have to be dusted off. There were hasty meetings of governors and premiers and ministers, and letters were soon on the way from Nova Scotia and New Brunswick. The Canadians would be welcome at the conference as unofficial observers.

From Prince Edward Island the reply was longer in coming, and for good reason. No Islander would consider crossing the Strait to attend this unlikely conference. If it were held, they hinted with adamant politeness, it must certainly be held at Charlottetown. On July 29, as tolerant larger brothers, Tupper and Tilley agreed. Telegrams went out naming Charlottetown as the site of the conference and September 1 as the date for its beginning.

There remained the selection of delegates, and the names were soon made public. With John Hamilton Gray for Prince Edward Island there would be Coles, Palmer, A. A. Macdonald, and Pope. With Tupper for Nova Scotia there would be two affable lawyers from his own side of the House, W. A. Henry and R. B. Dickey, and there would be Archibald and McCully from the party across the aisle. Coming with Tilley from New Brunswick would be a namesake of the Prince Edward Island premier, another John Hamilton Gray, who was a thoughtful and eloquent lawyer. There would be Edward Barron Chandler who was widely respected as an elder statesman of the province, W. H. Steeves, a hard-headed lumberman, and John Mercer Johnson, a rising politician who was an enthusiast for new causes. Tilley, like Tupper and Gray, had carefully balanced political friends and enemies. If any new cause should emerge at Charlottetown the risks would have to be shared.

There was a burst of talk in the newspapers, all lukewarm and much of it suspicious. The Canadians were given no credit for their coming. Whatever they brought, it was not likely to be welcome and they had promised nothing at all. There would be one prospective delegate conspicuous by his absence. Joseph Howe, replying to a stiff little note from Tupper, had quite as stiffly declined to attend the meeting.

4

Charlottetown

THROUGH AUGUST the Canadians in coalition were busy at Quebec. They had agreed to devise a plan of federal union. Now they must do it. They must resolve their old enmities, suspend their fears and suspicions and agree, at least in principle, on the central hopes that joined them.

On every hand they were faced by contradictions. In every man the old fears lurked and the old certainties maintained their grip. To Brown it had been inevitable that in any nation of the future the English should prevail. To Cartier it had been intolerable. Over that gulf Macdonald had hung suspended, and even Galt's dreams of railways and widening riches had not bridged it. It could only be bridged by men of a new view, by these same men looking with new eyes. Gradually they had come to do so, and it was Brown who had changed first.

He had stood up before his committee on that first May morning, a man wearied of politics and scarred by incessant battle. It had seemed a battle to extinguish the French. He had never regarded it so. It had been for him a battle of Protestant Englishmen to grow in their own way. To all this the French of the other province, with their differing laws, their separate education, their 'foreign' tongue, their omnipresent Church, had seemed an insuperable bar. Yet must they be? That was the new thought. He had longed for the nation of a whole people, one people. Could there be two, instead, going their way together?

It was that question they faced directly now, Brown and the other men. On one rock they stood; they wished to be British subjects. That was the breath of life to Brown and Macdonald, opposites though they were in too much else. Galt had sometimes wavered when the mind of the man of business ranged over the continent and measured the vast achievements of the United States. He had supported, years before, a movement to join the Union, but that was over now. Cartier's rebellious thoughts had been laid away with his youth. He had seen that the great democracy, the great melting-pot, could only swallow the French as a separate people. Under the Crown they had lived a life of their own, thus far. But what of this new prospect, this new Brown?

He had begun with the cry of 'justice for Upper Canada', and it was still his first thought. It was Cartier's first fear. Justice for Upper Canada meant Representation by Population, the dominance of the new union by an Upper Canadian majority. Would Lower Canada accept it, whatever the promise or plan? Never, Cartier knew, if the two old partners were simply joined again with the English ruling at last. There were too many rancorous memories, too much old distrust. The hope lay with the men of the Maritime colonies, another million English who were not Upper Canadians. If they joined, the balance of union would change. Would they sometimes counter the strength of the Upper Canadians, throw their weight with the French? It was a hope slender and treacherous enough, but now there had begun to be others. There was the new spirit in Brown, there was the promise of new safeguards in this Federal form of union.

Each of the partners, though joined by a central parliament, would live to itself in much and would be conceded its own powers. Here was the great difference and the test of the new spirit. What powers would this man of the dominant English concede to the French minority? Gradually this grew clear. He would concede all that was necessary to their dignity as an equal people. In a Lower Canada separate from Upper Canada the old and tyrannous fears would be relaxed. Dominance would stop short. There would be common strength and shelter under the Crown. There would be common goals. But there would not be the common schools that Brown had fought for, centrally controlled and everywhere the same. He had seen them as the moulds to shape a nation, to make its peoples one and make them English. Now, he had yielded. The French might teach their children as they wished, shape their lives as they wished. So might the English. In each province education would be separate and separately controlled. In neither province would it be used to compel a people. The right of each minority to its schools, English or French, would be guaranteed, inviolable. All this Brown had conceded, and on all this the hope of union turned.

It brightened day by day as Galt marshalled the complexities of finance and nation-building and Macdonald warmed to the work – his swift, deft mind playing over the machinery of government, searching out flaws, weighing new means. He was still the least at ease, the least convinced, the man most dubious of the plan. The old union had failed; he had no wish to restore it. But he saw in Federal union a cluster of states, straining their separate ways and straining apart. He saw new freedoms but he saw no strength. He was the friend of Cartier and the friend of the French. He was readier than Brown to concede what Brown conceded. He could see as far and dream as high as Galt, but the more he looked to the future the more he felt the need of a central purpose driving a new nation. There must be a single mind, a British mind; he was wholly sure of that. He was doubly sure as he watched the American union, torn by the conflict of its many minds.

Seventy-seven years ago the Americans had sat down, as these British sat here now, to frame a constitution. It had been a great and mighty work, yet it seemed to have failed in the end. It had not been equal to the strains of the years, the pull of the warring wills, the needs of growth. What had been done wrong? He thought he saw the answer. The states had come together like jealous sovereigns, granting a tithe of power to central government, naming those powers, limiting them forever. It should be the other way round. The central power should grant what must be granted. It should name the rights and powers of separate provinces, keeping all else to itself. All powers unnamed should reside with the central government, common to the nation and the core of its strength. There was the reserve to meet the years ahead, to deal with the strains and problems growth would bring.

It was a plan for today, perhaps a plan for tomorrow. It would give security to Cartier's French. It might meet the other demands of the sea-side colonies. Provinces would come together diverse and free, but they would come with freedoms granted by central power. Might they come one day to merge those common freedoms, repose those separate wills in the greater will? Macdonald did not know, he could only hope. He would have liked another plan, but there was none. He would take this, then, and shape it as he could, working with these others while he thought beyond them.

The plan took form as the summer neared its end, and in George Brown a kind of wonder grew. He had been a bachelor till he was forty-three. Now he was the adoring husband of Anne Brown and the adoring father of two-year-old Maggie. He had been fretful of absence from them and restless in hot Quebec. In

his endless letters he had sometimes written derisively
of all the talk, and sometimes complacently of the old
enemies he had forced to the conference table. But
enemies and friends were fellow workmen now and
the tone of the letters had changed. 'It will be a
tremendous thing if we accomplish it,' he wrote to
Anne after one of the later meetings. 'I don't believe
any of us appreciate the immensity of the work we
are engaged in.'

By August 29 all the Canadians could do for the
moment was done. The plan was made. Cartier and
Brown had given each other their trust, with one grim
proviso. Whatever the fate of the plan, Brown had
made clear, there could be no turning back. In this
union or another, with the French or in spite of them,
Upper Canada would have its way, its due political
power. A failure now would mean a new union of the
Canadas alone, or the breaking up of the Canadas.
There would be another confrontation in the ancient
war of the peoples and this time, perhaps, the last.

The hope lay in the Maritimes. With that hope,
towards the end of the August day, they prepared
themselves for their journey. There would be Brown
and Cartier, Macdonald and Galt. There would be
the handsome William McDougall who supported
Brown, and the reticent Hector Langevin who was
always Cartier's man. There would be the patient Scot
from Kingston, Alexander Campbell, who was Macdonald's partner in law and friend in many troubles.
Best known of all to the hosts waiting below would be
the little elfin Irishman, Thomas D'Arcy McGee. He

and his hundred friends had preached and pleaded and joked a year before in the cause of union. He would discover now if the seed had taken root.

It was early evening when the eight well-groomed gentlemen boarded the *Queen Victoria*, their little ship of destiny. It lay in the river below the rock of Quebec, scrubbed, provisioned, and painted for its voyage to Prince Edward Island. Its sides shivered a little as the engines began to throb, its bright deck-awnings fluttered in the last of the slanting sunlight and it started down the St. Lawrence.

Charlottetown lay ahead, with its seven thousand people, its few white mansions sheltered by the last stands of oak or pine or elm, and its rows of small brown houses running straight to the water's edge. It was a town throbbing with excitement, but hardly the excitement that statesmen might have wished. Islanders were in no mood to make history. The travelling circus had arrived for its annual visit, and through four afternoons and evenings most of the people and most of their legislators went streaming out to the big tent. They were not at the harbour on the afternoon of August 31 when a boat came in with the delegates from Nova Scotia. Charles Tupper and his party found no preparations made for them and only W. H. Pope, elegant and polite but embarrassed by the lack of colleagues, to help in their search for lodgings. For Tilley and his men from New Brunswick, who arrived at eleven that night, there was even less ceremony. They found, they reported, only 'neglect and indifference . . . measured out to them . . . with beautiful impartiality'.

In the graceful Colonial Building next morning, ruffled and rumpled men who had slept badly were presented at last to their hosts for the Maritime conference. It was not a promising meeting. Archibald and McCully were uneasy enough to be here at the side of Tupper, and with Tupper's friends. In Tilley's delegation there were colleagues of the moment who were usually political enemies and might soon be enemies again. There was small reassurance for any of the mainland men in the stiff politeness of John Hamilton Gray, the Island's premier. The young A. A. Macdonald seemed friendly enough and Pope was earnestly affable, but it was George Coles and Edward Palmer who towered over them, measuring and watchful. There was a great deal of watchfulness in all of the delegations, and very little enthusiasm. Politicians smelt danger. They were here, after all, rather in spite of themselves and forced here by Canada. Each of them had the air, as he took his seat at the table, of a man who would like to be elsewhere.

Colonel Gray, as chairman, declared the conference open. Discussion began and went on, vague and strained, circling the lack of a plan. The project of Maritime union would not come to life. The delegates were waiting and they all knew it, though no man there could admit it. Shortly before noon W. H. Pope excused himself and retired. The show of business could go along without him, and the *Queen Victoria* was steaming up Hillsborough Bay. The Canadians would have to be met.

As Pope came down to the harbour the ship was rounding in and dropping its anchor smartly. It was impressive and intended to impress, but the lack of an audience was painful. Only a few dockside idlers were watching in the warm sunlight, and only a leaky oyster-boat was available by the quays. The bearded Provincial Secretary, dressed in his official best, climbed into the boat, seated himself on a barrel, and pointed to the *Queen Victoria*. The boat's owner obligingly rowed him out.

If it was a disconcerting reception for the men come down from Canada, they did not intend to show it. They could not afford to. They had much to accomplish, many suspicions to dispel, and they had come carefully equipped. 'Having dressed ourselves in correct style,' reported George Brown to his Anne, 'our two boats were lowered man-o-war fashion and each being duly manned with four oarsmen and a boatswain, dressed in blue uniform, hats, belts, etc. in regular style, we pulled away for shore and landed like Mr. Christopher Columbus who had the precedence of us in taking possession of portions of the American continent.'

It began to seem, even by the end of that day, that George Brown's exuberant simile had contained a germ of truth. The Canadians were ushered in on the Maritime conference, and the conference promptly adjourned. For men come as observers there was nothing to observe. Nor was there any business for the rest of the afternoon. The 'shake-elbow and how d'ye do' was followed by the disposal of delegates in their lodgings and then a dinner in the evening at Government House. There was only bustle and blandness and a rash of official greetings, yet something stirred through it all. The Canadians seemed to be here with a sense of purpose. The Maritimers were wary but they were curious and eager too.

On the next morning, Friday, September 2, all the delegates gathered in the same council-room to hear the plan of union. For the next three days, with a Sunday in between, the Canadians stood before them, changed men, changing their listeners. The Maritimers had known of Macdonald as the shifty politician, only firm in his dread of federal union. Now he proposed it, earnestly and openly, as the one salvation of Canada and the best hope of the Maritimes. Apart they were all nothing, together they could be strong. They could avoid the faults and flaws of the American union; he showed them how. He showed them the better, he was all the more impressive, because he had come so painfully himself, and with so many reservations, to support the plan before them.

Cartier spoke next, the vivid little Frenchman who had seemed the apostle of discord. His staccato English rasped them, they were quite at a loss with some of his mangled phrases, yet he drove his point home. The French no less than the English wished to be part of a nation. They wished for a door on the sea, a way to the west, a shared greatness. They wished for a life to be lived by all in common and under an English king. They were prepared to build, to sacrifice, to take enormous risks, always remaining themselves. On this plan, sharing the risks and sacrifices, they had made their peace with Brown.

Brown rose at his side, confirming the pact, widening the scope of the plan. The nation he spoke for would be a nation of English and French. It would be changed in much from the old shape of his hopes, but his hopes were wiser now. They were greater and they were nearer; they were as near as this very day because they were now shared by Cartier.

Impressive as any words was the sight of Brown himself, the grim, embattled Protestant at the side of the French Canadian. Gulfs had been bridged here, old walls were giving way. Then Galt stood up and other walls went down. First was the wall of the wilderness dividing Canada from the sea. The first task of the union would be a railway linking the colonies. The little colonial tariffs would be swept away, trade would flow free. Six colonies would be one, sharing the common wealth, building on common strength, opening out vistas never known before. He spoke of facts with figures in his hand, yet charged them with some magic of his own. Men cramped in littleness saw bigness beckon. They heard that railway-whistle once again, shrill in the far-off Rockies.

The Canadians had made their case and it was won. Dissenting voices rose and fell away, stilled by the end of a week and gladly stilled. Objections died, excitement took their place, even in the delegates who had hoped for least. The hard, brusque, reckless power of Tupper was thrown to the plan, forcing the wind he had raised and then forgotten. It was blowing a gale now, and carrying Tilley with it. Even the islanders were swaying forward. They had caught the gleam of the shores beyond the Strait. They had glimpsed the money to buy their landlords out. Their skies were sunny and their smiles were warm as high debate gave way to jovial banquets and the conference came to its end.

The rest was travelling and crowds and speeches. The Canadians must be seen in the lands they had won. The delegates went to Halifax, they went to Saint John and Fredericton, everywhere toasted at enormous dinners, everywhere deafened by the ring of cheers. They had come to apathy and wrought a miracle; they had found Excalibur in a stagnant pond. 'For twenty long years,' said John A. Macdonald to his hosts in Halifax, 'I have been dragging myself through the dreary waste of Colonial politics. I thought that there was no end, nothing worthy of ambition, but now I see something which is well worthy of all I have suffered.'

Then it was time for home and for recovery. In less than a month the delegates would meet again, this time in Quebec. The breathless hope must be hammered into fact.

5
Quebec

ON THE MORNING of October 10, 1864 the men who had attended the conference in Charlottetown assembled again in Quebec. With them now were ten additional delegates, including two from Newfoundland. The fourth of the Maritime colonies was at last interested and would be well represented here by a pair of its ablest men. Frederic Bowker Terrington Carter, a lawyer, and Ambrose Shea, a merchant, were both members of old island families who had many ties with England. Yet, though they opposed each other in politics, they were men of the new world and the promise of Charlottetown excited them. Carter deplored the fact that rich Newfoundlanders retired to England to spend their fortunes. 'I look to Federation,' he said, 'as opening up a wide field for enterprise in this Continent.' Shea hoped for the time when a fleet of steamships would link the island to the mainland. 'We have what Canada requires,' he said, 'and we want the class of goods that Canada can supply.'

For Prince Edward Island, Colonel Gray was still eloquently hopeful and was still strongly supported by W. H. Pope and A. A. Macdonald. Edward Palmer and George Coles had begun to have second thoughts, but their weight was now balanced by that of two new men. T. H. Haviland, a lawyer, seemed to be entirely of a mind with his Premier. 'As a British American,' he said, 'I will go heart and soul for a Federal Union of all the Colonies.' Edward Whelan, though not so enthusiastic, had the advantage of being a convert. As editor of one of Charlottetown's newspapers, and as a touchy Irish politician who had not been invited to the first conference, he had been sceptical and suspicious during the days at Charlottetown. He had changed now and was to change more as the arguments of the Canadians convinced him and the atmosphere of Quebec enfolded him.

Tupper had made no change in the group from Nova Scotia. Joseph Howe would be missing from Quebec as he had been missing from Charlottetown. When the delegates met on the island Howe had been cruising glumly in coastal waters, busying himself with fish. He had come home obviously in a bad mood, obviously feeling left out, and dismissing the work of the conference as idle talk. He had boasted fretfully that he could frame a better plan himself in a few hours, he saw no purpose in a second meeting at Quebec, and in any case he 'would not play second fiddle to that damned Tupper'. There was danger in all this and Tupper was well aware of it. But his government was firmly in power and he was well pleased with the growing rapport between himself, Henry and Dickey on the one hand and Archibald and Mc-Cully on the other. Howe's friends were moving with the times if Howe was not. Party feuds were settling into the background as five Nova Scotians together became gripped by the idea of union.

Tilley was less happy with the state of affairs at home. He had no great enemy but he was not so sure of his friends. The term of his government, moreover, was nearing its end. It was not strong, and there would soon have to be an election. If union became an issue it was certain to be a dangerous one, with politicians torn between the divided interests of the province. There would be the allurements of Maine competing with the promise of Canada, there would be suspicion of the French, there would be Americanism at war with Britishness and there would be the simple dread of change. With all this in mind he had added two strong figures to his delegation. Peter Mitchell, lawyer, lumberman, and shipbuilder, was gruff, masterful, and cross-grained, certain to be a difficult colleague. But he wanted a railway with Canada and he would work for it. Charles Fisher was a man to have on one's side, a supple and skilful lawyer and a master politician. These two, with Chandler, Gray, Steeves, and Johnson, would be powerful support in any coming battle if they could all be held together.

SIR ETIENNE PASCHAL TACHE

For the Canadas there were now twelve men in place of eight, with two new-comers from each section. James Cockburn of Upper Canada was a sober Scottish lawyer and one of Macdonald's oldest and firmest supporters. Oliver Mowat, the second Upper Canadian, had begun his career as a law student in Macdonald's office but had moved away from his master in the direction of George Brown. Yet neither man had dominated him, nor ever would. Chunky and small, with shrewd and studious eyes peering out from behind steel-rimmed spectacles, he could be counted on here to think and speak for himself.

From Lower Canada there was Jean-Charles Chapais, a merchant who had gone into politics and made 'honest as Chapais' a proverb in his home county. Modest and silent as Langevin, he was wholly loyal to Cartier and made few claims for himself. Towering over him was the venerable and kindly figure of Sir Etienne-Pascal Taché, who was now meeting with the delegates for the first time. The only one of them who wore a knighthood, Taché was an ailing man with less than a year to live. He had hoped to retire after a long life in politics, but had been called back when the coalition was formed to serve as its formal head. Cartier, Macdonald, and Brown, no one of whom would give precedence to the other, would all give precedence to him. Amiable, conciliatory, and respected alike by French and English, he was to preside over the conference.

The thirty-three men who would one day come to be known as the Fathers of Confederation were now

together. Twenty of them were lawyers and three
were journalists. There were four merchants and two
doctors. There was Gray of Prince Edward Island, the
former soldier, Tilley the former druggist, Galt the
financier, and George Coles the brewer. They were
young men as politicians go. Taché, the oldest among
them, was sixty-nine. A. A. Macdonald, the youngest,
was thirty-five. There were three more in their thirties,
sixteen in their forties, eleven in their fifties, and only
one man beside Taché – Edward Barron Chandler of
New Brunswick – who had passed his sixtieth birthday. Of the men who stood out as leaders, Cartier was
fifty, John A. Macdonald was forty-nine, Galt was
forty-seven, Brown and Tilley were each forty-six,
and Tupper was forty-three. Greater and lesser alike,
they were vigorous, ambitious men – a broad, rich
section of the best brains of the country. All too often
they had been pitted against each other. Now for a
moment enmities were in suspension, hope was high
and purpose guided politics.

They had come, some of them with wives and some
with wives and daughters, many to see Canada for
the first time. They had not been provided with the
lovely weather of Charlottetown, for Quebec's golden
October had failed to arrive this year. Delegates and
their women-folk had been greeted with sheets of
rain driven on a chill wind, but they had found much
to make up for it. Many of the Maritimers had come
by the *Queen Victoria* which had been sent down the
river to bring them. All were established now in the
freshly-decorated suites of the handsome St. Louis

51

Hotel, marvelling at the attentive service and the length of the mighty menus. Each day, as George Brown informed his Anne, the visitors would 'sit down to a "company dinner" of the first class'. There was the promise before them also of elaborate balls and receptions, for the Canadian guests of Charlottetown were determined here to be graceful and lavish hosts. Yet at the centre of all was a hard core of business. These men were in earnest. They looked out the rain-splashed windows of the Legislative Building at the grey sweep of the St. Lawrence. They were assembled on the cliff of Quebec, with all its memories. Once more this rock, so near to every heartbeat of their history, was to be a scene of decision.

Their chairs were waiting for them, closely ranked around the long table covered with its red cloth. They settled into their places, with Taché at the middle as chairman. There was a little speech of welcome and there were little speeches in reply. Procedures and methods of voting were discussed and settled. Then John A. Macdonald moved, seconded by Leonard Tilley, 'that the best interests and future prosperity of British North America will be promoted by a federal union under the Crown of Great Britain, provided such union can be effected on principles just to the several provinces'. The conference was launched.

It was to go on for seventeen days, through most of which incessant, unseasonable rain drummed at the windows. The cold wind blew outside and rivulets of muddy water coursed down the steep, cobbled, crazily winding streets of the old city. In ante-rooms and corridors newspaper reporters from Canadian and Maritime cities and even one or two from the United States and England lay in wait for the delegates, resenting the closed door and the veil of determined secrecy that surrounded all the debates. As each day's meeting ended committees and delegations hurried away to convene for separate sessions in private rooms, hammering out new resolutions, debating new strategy. There were waves of angry despondency as the rocks of discord rose, separating hard-faced men. There were moments of high accord, and moments of reluctant yielding, as the rocks moved. Then in the wind-blown darkness of the streets there was the nightly glitter of carriages, the clip-clop of splashing hooves and the blaze of welcoming doorways. Whatever the day had brought, the night brought dancing. The bright torrents of the women's gowns flowed inward, always accompanied by the statesmen's broadcloth. There was never an evening without its festive occasion. Everyone had to be entertained, everyone took a hand in it, and everyone seemed to enjoy it.

To pretty young Mercy Coles, daughter of George Coles, it was to be a time of frustration. She was not interested in politics, she had come for the balls and parties, and she was soon in bed with a cold. Doctor Tupper often looked in on her and was always the soul of kindness. Other delegates called to prescribe their favourite remedies. Hewitt Bernard, Macdonald's private secretary and the secretary to the conference was polite, attentive, and amusing till he came down with the gout. She regretted his absence

then and was not at all concerned, as posterity would
be later, at the fact that the minutes of the conference
became sketchy. When she felt well enough to return
to the round of parties she encountered John A. Macdonald. He was an 'old humbug', as she had probably
learned from her father, but she found him funny and
delightful and full of solicitous bustle, hurrying away
at suppertime to see that she got her dessert. She
laughed at D'Arcy McGee who was sometimes in his
cups. She was amazed at Cartier's dancing and delighted with his French folk songs, but always the
rain came back and *la grippe* with it. Nor did she find
that the mood of her father improved as the days and
nights of the conference lengthened out.

For Edward Whelan, on the other hand, Quebec
was soon to become enchanted ground. He had come
from Charlottetown, a loyal Islander, promising the
readers of his newspaper full and frank reports. He
found, perhaps with relief, that he was bound to
secrecy as a delegate and could only hint in his letters
at the course of the high arguments. He was soon too
tired in any case, and too filled with wonder, to go
into much detail. 'If the Delegates will survive the
hospitality of this great country,' he wrote on the
second day, 'they will have good constitutions – perhaps better than the one they are manufacturing for
the Confederation.'

Disgusted with the weather and troubled for a
while by the 'mazy, crooked, narrow and bewildering
streets', he sprinkled his first reports with a tincture
of acid. He noted at the Governor General's reception

'the almost universal tendency to corpulency' of the ladies of Quebec. 'I have seen more pretty girls at a Government House ball in Charlottetown,' he declared, 'than I was able to see among the gorgeously dressed belles of Quebec.' Yet he was already yielding to the subtle aura of the great. Lord Monck, the Governor General, he found, 'converses in a free-and-easy, matter-of-fact style, same as any sensible man; so that if his companion is not a born fool he need not be impressed by any of that stupid awe which fools sometimes feel in the presence of a live Lord.'

Two nights later came the Ministerial Ball, 'a stunning, crushing affair' held in the Legislative Building. Every window of the great house by the river blazed with light, every room was alive with colour, while the music for quadrilles, lancers, polkas, and waltzes floated from two ballrooms. 'I will not attempt to give a minute description,' Whelan wrote breathlessly. 'The bewildering scene baffles all my descriptive powers . . . let the reader fancy that he is elbowing his way from the House of Assembly to the Council Chamber with all its rich paintings – he sees two floors occupied incessantly from 9 in the evening until 4 in the morning – beautiful women are floating past you everywhere in all the rich trappings of fashion – numerous gay officers in uniform, some of them exhibiting on their breasts Royal decorations given for distinguished merit – here is grace, loveliness and politeness at every step you take.'

The girls of Charlottetown heard no more talk of 'corpulency'. Quebec's women now seemed 'ten times more attractive', and the mingling of languages had become a joy to hear. He was delighted by the sight of 'the gay, garrulous and polite Frenchman (or French lady, if you will) gesticulating with hands and head, striving to make the Englishman or Irishman or Scotsman (who does not know a word of French any more than he knows Sanscrit) comprehend a strange jumble of French and excessively bad English. The French ladies here give a delightful tone to society. There is infinite grace of manner and faultless politeness ... they make no difficulty about falling in love – or seeming to fall in love – with a dozen gentlemen at a time.'

'Invitations both public and private are being poured in upon the delegates,' he reported on October 15, and by the 19th he had decided 'to be somewhat reticent hereafter regarding the social parties in which the Delegates engage, lest it should be supposed they do nothing else but frolic.' Yet he could not keep his promise in 'this gay, ancient and fascinating city' where 'it must require a small fortune to furnish out a lady's wardrobe – dresses all made of the richest materials and different on every occasion.' He marvelled, like Mercy Coles, at the energies of the great and tried, though not very hard, to explain their gaiety on grounds of policy. 'The Cabinet Ministers, the leading ones especially ... do not seem to miss a dance during the livelong night. They are cunning fellows and ... know that if they can dance themselves into the affections of the wives and daughters of the country the men will certainly be an easy conquest.'

Between the races conquest seemed to be reciprocal. At a private ball given by the wealthy Tessiers there were more French than British, but 'conversation was carried on with the English and Irish, who have all determined upon studying French forthwith'. Yet at another ball, Whelan declared, he had been assured by Sir Etienne-Pascal Taché himself that 'the time will come – not indeed in the present generation, nor perhaps in the next – when the French element will be absorbed into the English one; but that result must be brought about by time, and not by the violent action of politicians.' All things indeed seemed to have become possible, at least to Edward Whelan, as he finally came to beg for his readers' prayers 'to the end that we may be removed from this dear, charming, abominable, killing, pleasure-ridden city before the winter shall have set in, otherwise the undertaker will effect our removal for us'.

Edward Palmer, his fellow delegate, was to say later that Whelan had spent too much time writing notes for his newspaper to be aware of what was going on at the conference. It may well have been true. The brilliant evenings did not solve the problems. The thirty-three men came back to them day by day, sometimes the worse for wear and always to face new difficulties. Debate grew sharp as hopes and facts collided. The sheen of the easy promises that had been made or hinted at in Charlottetown was soon rubbed away. The rasp of fears and jealousies began to be heard. The Maritime colonies had been proud and petty sovereignties. Their delegates winced now at the claims that union would impose, even this federal union. They would be dwarfed by numbers, linked with Frenchness, drawn by the mighty pull of inland power. Where did it lead to? What must they give up?

Cartier and Brown had come to a broad agreement. Yet what did agreement mean when put in practice? How were the wheels of government to turn, separate and apart for the separate concerns of peoples, yet always meshing where the peoples were one? They had abandoned the blunt simplicities of the old union. British and French alike were yielding much. Where was the gain to balance what they would lose?

The answers slowly came, for the Maritimes and the Canadas alike. Debating around the long table, huddled in separate committees, or munching together in the little ante-room during the fifteen minutes they allowed themselves for lunch, the delegates cleared the way to the central facts. They were giving up little they could hope to hold much longer. The Canadas could not return to their old condition. In all but name they were separate again, hungry for growth, shadowed by new fears, waiting the outcome of the Civil War and dreading the forces that the war would loose. The Maritime colonies had lived as the wards of England with their backs turned to the continent, and that must soon end. The mother wished it and the times compelled it; they must stand on their own feet.

Where should they turn to make a life for themselves? The natural way, for them as for the Canadas, had always led to the Americans. It was traced by the rivers and mountains, the shape of the land, the course of settlement, the flow of trade. Everything drew together north and south, everything men could see and hold and count. Yet against it stood the old, invisible wall, the stubborn wish to be British. Holding that wish, they were bound a common way. Their road led west from the sea along the river.

They must take to the road together or not at all. That great imperative bore the obstacles down. Brown's cause was gained; Cartier's conceded. Macdonald sketched the supple form of union, supple himself, and never quite content. He never would be content with this federal plan. It was still for him an American league of states, of separate powers at odds with central power. Yet he had gained his all-important point; this would be a plan without the American weakness. Provinces should have their powers and freedoms defined. All else resided in the central power. He looked to that power, though he did not say so, to shape the future nation to his hopes.

Galt rose to deal with railways and with money. First there would be that steel link to the sea; it was the spine of union. Then there was wealth to share, and also debts. They must both be pooled and parcelled out again, with richer colonies assisting poorer. There would be no tariffs dividing colonies now; a single tariff would embrace the union. The revenues lost would be replaced by grants, each to a colony as predetermined, governed by population. Here there was long debate and always would be; money was money. Prince Edward Island, with landlords on its mind, could get no promise from Galt to buy them out. The smiles of Charlottetown grew faint and strained; Islanders looked grim. Yet over them all the greater promise glowed; the burly hopes of Tupper rode down fears. Dissent hung, lingering, but debate was stilled.

The other rocks rose up, to be washed over. What was the form that government should take? There were no lords here to fill a House of Lords yet all men felt the need of such a place, a home of strong and seasoned elder statesmen living above the cries of mobs and parties. It was framed at last, one day to be the Senate, promised a power it would never have. The greatest body would be the House of Commons, home of the central power. It must be filled by freely-elected men, chosen in due proportion from each of the provinces. What was the number and the due proportion? The work began to find a measuring-stick. It emerged at last, simple as it was sound, pivoting on George Brown's rule of population. Lower Canada would retain its sixty-five constituencies. Upper Canada, in proportion, would be given eighty-two. For Nova Scotia there would be nineteen, for New Brunswick fifteen, for Newfoundland eight, and for Prince Edward Island five. Once more the qualms of smallness stirred debate. The Islanders looked grimmer than before and even the mainland Maritime men were shaken. Yet facts were facts and figures had their way. The parliament and its basis were established. They were nearly done. The seventy-two articles of the Confederation Scheme had been drawn up. There was to be a federation of six provinces, each with its local government under a general government. English and French would be equally official languages in the federal parliament and the federal courts, as well as in the courts and legislature of the home province of the French. A railway was to tie the Canadas to the sea. Nor was that all. One cloudy afternoon, on a late day of the conference, they had framed the resolution that contained within the dry shell of its words the greatest promise of Howe. The communications with the Territories, it provided, 'and the improvements required for the development of the Trade of the Great West . . . shall be prosecuted at the earliest possible period that the state of the Finances will permit.'

On October 27 the conference came to its end. The thirty-three men had captured the age-old dream. They had framed their union 'just to the several provinces'. They were hoarse with debate, wrung dry by hard thought, exhausted by hard festivities, and they were not yet finished. Before them still was a great tour of the Canadas that would carry them west to the Lakes. They were hailed by the crowds of Montreal and Toronto. They came to Ottawa, the dismal wilderness lumber town unhopefully chosen seven years before as the least unlikely capital of a province always divided. While Lower Canada quarrelled with Upper Canada and Toronto vied with Quebec as the seat of government, the new parliament buildings rising in Ottawa had seemed grotesquely magnificent, never likely to be occupied. They did not seem so now. They seemed to reflect the promise these visitors brought. In the picture-gallery of the noble central pile, the only room roofed-over, the delegates lunched and delivered themselves of speeches. They were the first speeches to be heard in this house and they were met with wild applause. 'We were received like conquerors,' said Henry of Nova Scotia, 'like warriors returning from a great victory.' But Henry was far from home when the cheers resounded, and victory was much more distant than it seemed.

6
Changing Winds

'THE TASK to which these provinces are called is no light or unimportant one; they are now laying the foundations of an Empire, of an Empire that may last as long as the human race and whose bounds shall extend from the cold and sterile coasts of Newfoundland to the noble hills and peaceful havens of Vancouver's Island.' So said the Halifax *Morning Chronicle* before the Quebec Conference began. 'Will the people . . . rise to the level of the occasion,' asked the Montreal *Gazette* when the conference was over, 'to settle the destiny of this northern country and the people that dwell here?'

That was the question now, and there were soon disquieting answers. The thirty-three men of Quebec had been hailed as prophets and builders and had replied with confident words. Yet they were all too well aware, not only of sullen murmurs beneath the cheers, but of private rifts and doubts. They were returning to face their legislatures with a huge and complex plan, and beyond those politicians lay the faceless mass of the people. Would the politicians rise to the level of the occasion? Would the people? Were they themselves, the delegates, at ease on these heights of statecraft?

The seventy-two resolutions of the Quebec Scheme, before they could take effect, must be separately approved by Canada, Nova Scotia, New Brunswick, Prince Edward Island, and Newfoundland. They must then be forwarded to the Colonial Office in London as a request to the Queen for union. That granted, an Act of the Imperial Parliament must make the union. It was a long road planned to be a high road, over the heads of the people. This project could not be allowed to ramble by the dusty town halls and the country stumps, through all the clamour and clatter of general elections.

It would be urged that neither the delegates to Quebec nor the legislatures who appointed them had any authority to enact so sweeping a change. They were proposing to alter the lives of all their constituents; they should refer the question back to them. Yet how could the ordinary man understand the plan? How could he follow his legislator down this complicated and hazardous path, toward objectives and around pitfalls which the leader himself could only dimly see? How explain to him the meaning, purpose, and effect of each of those resolutions? That meaning and those effects must be summarized by the leaders, must be compressed and capsuled into taut and thrilling phrases. They must become the flags that marched at the head of the herd, and that way the herd must go. It must all be done 'at a bound' said John A. Macdonald, and often cynical though he was, he was not cynical in this.

As he came back from the conference and the routine of politics began again, everything was overshadowed by the great impending question. Yet in Upper Canada there was not much to fear. Macdonald's enemies would recall his opposition to the federal form of union. Brown would have to answer for his concessions to the French. Yet both could point to the collapse of the old union and the inevitability of change. They could point to the many gains for Upper Canada. There would be representation by population; the province of English Protestants would be dominant in the new parliament. It would be as free of the French in all its private concerns as the French were free of the English. Yet both would share the rich St. Lawrence basin and the link with the sea. They would turn, strengthened in common, for the march to the Great West.

Cartier must look at the other face of the pact. What Brown had gained he had given up. There was no denying the fact of those eighty-two members who would sit in the new House, facing the sixty-five from Lower Canada. Few French would be comforted by the thought of those other English, the new men from the Maritimes. They would see in the Great West, so near to Upper Canada, the all too likely promise of another English preserve. He could hear already the long roll of dissent, the cry that this union would be

65

the tomb of the French. Yet he had heard long before the glacier-slide of the times, the rumble of change. There was no resisting it, he had made his peace with it; he had done the best he could. He had imposed on Macdonald this federal form of union, he had wrung his safeguards from Brown, and the rest lay with the future. It would be a great future, a French and English future. It thrilled him; he would fight for it and win.

There was no such sureness in the men of the Atlantic colonies. Dissent had simmered there even in the midst of the conference, even through the cheers and speeches of the tour. It had been fought down and glossed over, it had been dissolved sometimes in the glamour of nation-building and concealed sometimes for the sake of mere politeness. Now, in the long, cold thoughts of a journey home, all of it came back. There was more of the same mood waiting ahead of it, and most on Prince Edward Island. It was there the storm broke first.

Cantankerous Edward Palmer returned to Charlottetown on the morning of November 9. He had taken pride, at Quebec, in referring to himself as 'the malcontent of the Conference', yet he had gone along on the tour with the other delegates and had even spoken hopefully. Now, with banquets and travel behind him, he became his dour self, convinced of his old convictions. He felt he had gone to Quebec with a promise or at least a half-promise that the new union, when made, would free Prince Edward Island from the grip of its British landlords. There was no

money for that in the seventy-two resolutions. Instead
there was the promise of sharing the mainland's debts,
in return for paltry grants. There was the promise of
a railway that would stop short at the far shore of
Northumberland Strait. It would not bridge those
waters but the arms of the union would. They would
reach across to ruffle the Island calm, alter the Island's
ways, dip in the Island's treasury. And what was
offered in return? Shadowy hopes that always looked
to the west, the complication of Frenchness, five
members, lost and ludicrous, in that House of Commons of 194. It was not to be, not while Palmer had
voice. Within one day of his return he was out in the
Market Square, using that voice.

He was first of the home-come Fathers to denounce
the child of his getting, but George Coles was close
behind him. He had bluntly warned the conference
on the first day at Quebec that without some strong
inducement 'we must not expect that Prince Edward
Island will come into a confederation to be taxed
three dollars per head instead of one dollar as at
present.' There was no such strong inducement, and
there was now wounded pride. An islander of islanders, Coles had always thought of Charlottetown as
the natural capital of any future union. 'Our Canadian
friends will be glad, I am sure,' he had once written
tolerantly, 'to spend a month or two in public business
here, if only to escape the fever and ague of their own
province.' He had found that his Canadian friends
had other ideas, and he had enjoyed his stay with
them less than daughter Mercy. The bigness of their

country depressed him and their claims left him aghast. Montreal city alone would have greater representation in the House of Commons than the whole of Prince Edward Island. The Island itself would be a mere tag to the mainland, 'a laughing stock to the world'.

George Coles was soon with Palmer, and A. A. Macdonald joined him. Haviland swayed to their side. Colonel Gray and the steadfast W. H. Pope remained committed to union, and Quebec City's most ardent admirer firmly supported them. Edward Whelan, now the travelled statesman and rich with his gorgeous memories, was acidly contemptuous of the 'small politicians' of 'this patch of sand bank in the Gulf of St. Lawrence'. Confederation, he was sure, would come about in spite of people 'who imagine they have such a paradise as would be contaminated by alliance with their powerful, prosperous fellow subjects on the mainland'. It was all to no purpose, however, and the 'small politicians' prevailed. In a short six weeks, with his delegation in shambles, Gray resigned as premier. The hopes of the Island's unionists went up on a dusty shelf.

Tupper and his Nova Scotians had come back of one mind, all with their reservations yet all firm for the plan. Money grants could be modified and other terms improved but the base of union would stand; they were wholly sure of that. They were not so sure of the mood of Joseph Howe, the unconsulted oracle. For years all thoughts of union had turned on this man. He had bred the thoughts and built up much of the province, he still stood for thousands as the symbol of its greatest age. He was older now, and out of office and bitter. He had been thrust aside by Tupper and he would not forget that. Yet here in this scheme of Quebec was almost his own plan, awaiting fulfilment at last. In Nova Scotia a word from Howe could make it. Yet another word might break it, and for long weeks there was only a brooding silence. Then, slowly and ominously, wheels began to turn.

The great merchants of Halifax were hardening against the scheme. That became obvious first and was not surprising. Their trade lay on the sea, to the east, not to the west. They did not like the prospect of western union, of tariff changes and tax changes; they were well enough as they were. They were powerful, dangerous, and hidebound, yet they could change; they could still be convinced if the proper voice were raised. It did not come. Instead, Jonathan McCully lost his job. He had come back, the delegate of Quebec, maker of the plan of union, burly and confident and probably swaggering a little. From his desk at the *Morning Chronicle* he had clouted the enemies of union in daily editorials. 'We have no sympathy with that class of man whose mental vision is bounded by Dartmouth on the one side and Citadel Hill on the other. It is not the building of a Town-house we are discussing; we are engaged in laying the foundations of an Empire.' He was still so engaged, in the early days of January, when he was invited to vacate his chair.

William Annand, the owner of the *Morning Chron-*

icle, was a lifelong friend of Howe. There was sign
enough in that. So far as McCully was concerned, the
change was not serious. Within two weeks he had
acquired his own newspaper and was going on as
before. But he was already a lesser voice, hardly
heard. On January 11, 1865, one day after the departure of McCully was announced, an unsigned letter
appeared in the *Morning Chronicle.* It was entitled
'The Botheration Scheme' and it was to be one of a
series. There was no signature necessary for only
Howe could have written it; the touch was unmistak-
able. So was the purpose. 'Of all the characters of
ancient story,' ran that first letter, 'the poorest-spirited
creature that we know is Esau; but if Nova Scotians
surrendered their powers of self-government and provincial independence for the precious mess of pottage
brought hither from Quebec, we would ever after be
held in deserved contempt.' There could be no more
doubt for Tupper and his fellow unionists. The weight
of the aging giant was thrown against them.

The troubles of Tilley in New Brunswick were also
mounting. He had come back, the head of a delegation pledged to union. But he was also head of a
government that had less than a year to live. He would
be forced by law to call an election in the spring. He
was expected, before that time, to secure the approval
of his legislature for the plan framed in Quebec. It
would have been difficult enough with the support of
a strong ministry; it soon became impossible with the
divided group he had.

Some of his ministers, who had not been delegates

to Quebec, opposed Confederation. Some of his delegates began to weaken, disturbed by the many questions raised at home. The old divisions and fears began to show. In this new union what would become of the powers of the local legislature? What would become of the office-holders' jobs? There would be new taxes imposed and old revenues lost and the grants in return would dribble from a central treasury, always far too small. The railway link with the Canadas was certainly a shining promise, but it was balanced by another promise. There was still that pull toward Maine, that talk of the 'Western Extension'. The great merchants of Saint John, like the great merchants of Halifax, were suspicious of union from the first. The railway line with Portland, promised by Western Extension, would feed their commerce into the American hopper. They were drawn to that; they were not drawn to Canada and not to Confederation. Tilley's cause faltered and his government crumbled under him while A. J. Smith, the leader of the opposition, stoked the fires of dissent. There was no course left but to call a general election, in spite of the protests in the mail from Canada.

The 'old humbug' who had amused Mercy Coles and failed to ensnare her father was anxiously watching the course of the general battle while he prepared for the one at home. Macdonald had expected trouble in Prince Edward Island. He saw that Tupper was in for a hard fight. But he had regarded New Brunswick as a 'safe' province and he was still for action at a bound. Tilley should press his resolution forward; he should act while he had the power. But the Upper Canadian was too far off from New Brunswick; he could not measure the difficulties and there was no room left for choice. By mid February the election was under way and in three grim weeks it was lost. Confederation was repudiated and Tilley was defeated even in his own constituency. For long months to come, as a leader without a seat, he would observe proceedings mournfully from a gallery of the House.

There remained Newfoundland, where Carter and Shea had returned soberly confident. For several years life on the island, always hard enough, had been doubly hard because of poor fishing and blighted crops. It seemed that union, with its prospect of mainland trade, offered new hope. 'We do not apprehend any serious difficulty in the passage of the Scheme in our Legislature,' wrote Shea, 'but it is not wise to be over-confident.'

It was not indeed. Poverty and hardship, it seemed, only bred fears and suspicions. Troubled men were not ready for new ventures, and a few rich men were ready to trade on their fears. Merchant magnates who had long ruled the island now found that Confederation would deprive Newfoundland of her right of 'independent legislation'. It would 'transfer the right of taxation from the people of this colony to the people of Canada'. Young Newfoundlanders, they solemnly warned, would be shipped abroad in some horrific future to fight the wars of Canadians.

The Newfoundland legislature opened on January 27, 1865 with an appeal for calm consideration of the

Quebec Scheme. But already outside the legislature the attack was under way. It mounted steadily, gaining strength with each mail from the other Maritime provinces. By the end of February Prince Edward Island had turned its back on the plan, Nova Scotia seemed marching away from it under the leadership of Joseph Howe, and Tilley was falling in New Brunswick. Even before he fell, support had collapsed in Newfoundland and the resolution in the legislature did not even come to a vote. Confederates had been brought to a stop, silenced and shaken.

Thus, by the early days of March, all four of the Maritime colonies seemed lost to the plan of union. But the stubborn idea would not die so easily. Against this sombre background the Canadians had begun their debate, and defeat in the sea-side provinces had not changed them.

7

Canada Decides

THE PARLIAMENT of Canada, under its coalition government, assembled at Quebec on January 19, 1865. On Friday, February 3, Sir Etienne-Pascal Taché rose to introduce the Quebec Resolutions. On Monday, February 6, debate began, with John A. Macdonald leading off for the government.

For nearly three months now the general shape of the plan had been common knowledge. There had been time for it to permeate the life of the province, to be studied by politicians and talked of by their constituents. Imperceptibly, and in spite of men, it had brought change already. Whatever the hopes or fears it might give rise to, everyone sensed the passing of old ways. Paralysis, parochialism, and littleness were somehow gone; the door once opened on a glimpse of great horizons would not be closed again. Yet the horizons were still far off, the distant goals were vague, and much closer at hand lay a cloud of doubts and enmities.

Brown had abandoned allies to enter this coalition. So had Macdonald. So had Cartier. They were resented and distrusted by those allies now. There was resentment over the meetings in Quebec, with all their secrecy. There was doubt above all, even by the best-disposed, that thirty-three men, working for seventeen days, could produce a remedy for the ills of the past and chart a course for the future.

Yet that was what they had done, or they had done nothing. The result of their work lay before the House now, not as a proposal or a suggestion or a motion to be discussed and amended in the ordinary way of parliament. There could be no altering the terms of these resolutions. They must be accepted in total or rejected in total.

The delegates of the Canadas had made, in effect, a treaty with the delegates from the Maritimes. It was not to be hoped that perfection had been achieved, nor was agreement complete. There was not one delegate who had not given way on some points, who did not have certain fears. Yet he must stand by what was written or he must go down with it. He could not agree to the changing of a word. That would involve the agreement of all the colonies. It would involve a new conference, and a new conference was unthinkable. It grew more so day by day as the bad news came from the Maritimes, yet the urgency grew with it. The work of those seventeen days must be saved here or it was lost everywhere. 'It was only by a happy concurrence of circumstances,' said John A. Macdonald, 'that we were able to bring this great question to

75

its present position. If we do not take advantage of the time, if we show ourselves unequal to the occasion, it may never return.' There would be these resolutions or there would be no others; it was this treaty or none.

If there was arrogance in the way the project was advanced, the times had forced it. If there was risk, Macdonald had prepared himself to assume it. He was a man who had grown in the eight-and-a-half months since that first May morning in the committee room with Brown. His fears of the United States were sharper now. The Civil War was certainly close to its end, and the North more certainly hostile. There had been angry incidents along the American border, climaxed at last by open threats of invasion. They were wild threats at the moment, mostly by loud-mouthed generals who talked of disposing of Canada 'as a St. Bernard would throttle a poodle pup'. Yet official hostility had revoked treaties and threatened trade, while the Fenians grew more menacing. They were rebellious Irish who had come from a blighted homeland and transferred their hate of England to the British in North America. Hardened soldiers, many of them, they were emerging from Union armies, forming themselves into bands, talking of northward invasion. How would they be met if they came?

With these thoughts Macdonald stood up, a man convinced, a man who saw his way. There was no longer safety, alone, for any of the British colonies. There was no longer strength or will or money in England to risk war with the Americans for scattered scraps of territory. But there was the will to foster a British nation, responsive to men who wished to grow themselves, sharing the risks and cost. The mother-land wished to see this union made, and such a union she would surely defend. That was enough to quell the last of the doubts. Here, for Macdonald, was the first firm step. He would take it and accept the risks beyond it.

He did not deny the faults and flaws of the plan; he looked to mend them in the nation-to-be. He brushed aside the rebukes of old supporters. Yes, he had changed; he had learned as wise men learn. No, he would not admit the need of elections. He would not go back with this scheme to consult the people. The time for decision was now, the place was here. They, these men in parliament, were the leaders charged to lead, to judge, and to decide. 'If we do not represent the people,' he cried out, lifting that cool dry voice for a passionate moment, 'we have no right to be here. But if we do represent them we have a right to see for them, to think for them, to act for them; we have a right to go to the foot of the Throne and declare that we believe it to be for the peace, welfare and good government of the people of Canada to form of these provinces one empire, presenting an unbroken and undaunted front to every foe.'

On February 7 Cartier rose to speak, the old foe of the English. There were grim-faced Upper Canadians still across from him, many of them scarred by wounds that Cartier had given and many who still resented Cartier's power. Yet they were faced by a man who

77

had set that power at risk, and not with the English alone. Antoine-Aimé Dorion sat in this House, the greatest of Cartier's French-Canadian enemies. He was no enemy to the English; he had once drawn nearer to Brown than any man of his people, seeking to bridge the gulf that lay between them. He had failed, Brown had failed; and he saw betrayal now, by Cartier and Brown alike. So did the other Dorion in that House, Eric, his younger brother. So did others among the troubled French, the one-time followers of this man who spoke. Never now, could Cartier be sure of his place with his own people.

He faced them all, buoyant and confident, still. He had judged and acted and he would not change. He welcomed what would be gained for what was given. There would be 'the maritime element', the open door on the sea. There would be the link of the railway and the road to the Great West. All this would come with union. 'Shall we,' he asked of his own people and the other, 'be content to maintain a mere provincial existence when, by combining together, we could become a great nation?' He had feared George Brown, he had feared the Protestantism of Upper Canada, he had feared the English with their urge for domination. Yet he feared that union of the Americans more. There was democracy, the rule of the mob, the melting-pot that had swallowed a dozen races. Here was the British Crown, this new union, these new pledges and safeguards. 'Either we must obtain British North American Confederation or be absorbed in an American confederation.' Those were the alternatives as

Cartier saw them, and he had made his choice.

That same day, after Cartier, Galt spoke, smilingly apologetic. He must talk of taxes and tariffs, grants, and railways. It was a drab subject, he said, compared to 'the important political and philosophical questions which are involved in the Confederation of the British North American colonies'. Yet the House sat silent while that luminous mind played over the thickets of problems and dispelled them. No one could doubt the wish of this man of money to 'remove forever the great and crying evils and dissensions which have existed in Canada for the last ten years'. No one could doubt his belief 'that this machinery, however faulty it may be, will yet under Providence open up for this country a happy career'.

'I cannot help but feel,' said George Brown, rising on February 8, 'that the struggle of half a lifetime, the strife and discord and abuse of many years, are all compensated by the great scheme . . . which is now in your hands.' He was still no friend to Macdonald, and he made that clear enough. Yet he was firmly beside Macdonald in this work. He stood as the ally and the friend of Cartier, while old-time friends called up his old hard words. Yes, he had said them and was now eating them. Yes, he had yielded some of his dearest hopes. There was much he disliked in the plan, much he would always regret. Yet with the whole, the sum of the resolutions, he was vastly, eagerly content. 'Sir,' he cried out as his long speech marched to its end, 'it may be that some of us will live to see the day when a great and powerful people

79

Sir Alexander Tilloch Galt

may have grown up in these lands – when the bound-
less forests all around us shall have given way to
smiling fields and thriving towns – and when one
united government under the British flag shall extend
from shore to shore.'

A mighty battle of words had only begun. It would
go on for more than a month. The men of the coalition
had launched the debate powerfully and surely. They
were already sweeping the lesser men along with
them, gathering in the votes. Whatever the sins of the
past, said one follow-my-leader, whatever the wars
of Cartier, Macdonald, and Brown, they 'now occupy
the same wigwam . . . it is said the same blanket
covers them . . . and I am prepared to support them'.

Such votes would count and their power was soon
felt. But there was no such jovial acceptance from
stronger figures. 'It is impossible for me . . . not to feel
that I am opposed to powerful odds,' said frail little
Christopher Dunkin, rising on the night of February
27, but 'there is a character of hurry impressed on the
whole style of this debate. . . . It is idle to talk vaguely
about the maintenance of British connection or to go
into magnificent speculations about the probable
results of independence, or blindly to urge this scheme
as a sure preventative of annexation to the United
States. These cheap and easy generalities are thoroughly unreliable. The only question is, how is this
plan, in its entirety, going to work?'

He was an English scholar and lawyer who had
once been a tutor in Greek. He felt 'a sort of foregone
conclusion' working against him, but for four hours

on each of two successive evenings he struggled on
with his speech, faltering and sick, asking the forbearance of the House and generously receiving it. He
was a man of the Eastern Townships who lived with
the French in Quebec. He was a man utterly sincere,
recognized for what he was, as friendly as any man
there to progress and growth. Yet, 'I do not believe in
any of these violent and sudden changes which have
for their object the creation of something entirely
new. I fear this scheme is just of the character to prevent that slow, gradual, healthy development which
I would wish to see.'

Clause by clause, hour after hour, he subjected the
words of Quebec to the cold probing of the man of
law and letters. He found in them neither the sure
promise of defence against the United States, nor the
maintenance of the connection with Great Britain,
nor of balanced freedom for the French and English.
He was sceptical of Galt's figures and of Galt's optimism. He distrusted the talk of railways, and in the
loose-knit scheme of general and local governments
he pointed unerringly to the many difficulties future
men would discover. He was the scholar in his element, looking for precision and certainties where no
certainties could be, distrusting the leap in the dark,
distrusting haste. The thirty-three men of the Quebec
Conference had worked for seventeen days. 'As a
result of these seventeen days we have from these
thirty-three gentlemen a scheme of a constitution . . .
so perfect do they seem to regard their pet measure
that we must not take time to discuss it . . . Was there

ever a scheme of this magnitude . . . that had to be passed (the whole of it) at once or never?'

' "If 'twere done, 'twere well 'twere done quickly," ' interjected D'Arcy McGee from across the aisle, and subsided instantly as he and the House recalled that he was using the words of Macbeth preparing the murder of a king.

'The honourable gentleman,' said Dunkin with tired forbearance, 'is welcome to all he can make of his quotation.' There were many such exchanges and he had had the better of most of them as he came to the end of his speech. Yet, when he was finished, he had nothing else to propose. The faults of the plan lay clear for all to see, but there was no other plan.

Antoine-Aimé Dorion spoke, the seasoned politician of forty-eight. He had fought Cartier throughout his political life, yet he had worked as hard as Cartier for a way of life with the English. He did not find it here. Neither did Eric Dorion, the younger brother, the man of thirty-nine who looked like a boy. Frail as Dunkin, he had once defeated Dunkin for the seat he held in this House. He would not hold it long, he had barely a year to live, but to the last days of that year he would be what he had always been, the *enfant terrible*, the passionate champion of his people, witty and fierce in debate. They were strong men, these Dorions, standing with Dunkin now, and behind them in that House were half of the French members.

'Why are we engaged in discussing Confederation?' Eric Dorion asked, then answered his own question. A discredited government, tumbled out of power, had allied itself with Brown to cling to office. It had made this plan of union with the unknown men of the Maritimes, and what did union offer? Safeguards for the French? Of what value was the promise of Cartier in the face of an English parliament? Of what value were George Brown's concessions? How long would they last? George Brown wanted representation by population, English dominance, and that was what he would get.

The plan was spoken of as a federal union, a linking of provinces each with its separate rights. All the world knew that John A. Macdonald stood for the legislative union in which a central government would be supreme. Cartier could never openly agree to that, but it would come. The powers of the provinces were strictly limited in the plan; the power at the centre embraced all else and was open to every expansion in an unknown future. To call this federalism, said Eric Dorion, was 'nonsense and repugnant to truth. All is strength and power in the federal government, all is weakness, insignificance, annihilation in the local government. The autonomy of Lower Canada is menaced and placed at the mercy of a parliament of one hundred and ninety-four members.' The plan was merely 'a legislative union in disguise'. His brother icily agreed. 'It is evident,' said Antoine-Aimé, 'that it is intended eventually to form a legislative union of all the provinces.'

The scheme, said Eric, was advanced in the name of defence against the United States. How could there be new strength in the creation of an indefensible frontier sixteen hundred miles long? The plan would result in a country 'without its like under the sun. In geographical form it resembles an eel. Its length would be everything, its breadth nothing.' That Intercolonial Railway, so often promised before, was promised again, but there was no word as to the route of the line or the cost. There was the still wilder prospect of an interoceanic railway across three thousand miles of unknown wilderness to reach the territories of British Columbia. Who could believe in that? Everything about the scheme could be dismissed as the work of fools, or rogues, or both. 'These gentlemen,' said Antoine-Aimé Dorion, 'only found out that Confederation was a panacea for all evils, a remedy for all ills, when their seats as ministers were in danger. I see in it nothing but another railway scheme for the benefit of the few.'

The hard words and the high words did not change many positions. Dunkin could not be sure of a dozen allies. For every man of the French who stood with the Dorions another stood with Cartier. Yet even as debate went on the background darkened. The plan itself seemed collapsing with the weight of the news from the east. Prince Edward Island was gone, Newfoundland was shuffling away, and Nova Scotia rumbled with the angry dissent of Howe. Latest and least expected came the blow of March 4, a telegram from New Brunswick announcing the fall of Tilley. 'Will the honourable gentlemen go to England and press on the scheme under such circumstances?' asked Antoine-Aimé Dorion on March 6. 'I say that this scheme is killed. I repeat that it is killed.'

'Our intention,' came the grim reply of Macdonald, 'is to get the sanction of this House to the Address I have moved.' Canada seemed all but alone now, but the clock could not turn back. For five days more he forced debate along, and at half-past four on the morning of March 11 the end came. Twenty-one French remained of the mind of the Dorions and twelve English with Dunkin, but their voice was overwhelmed. While a wild spring blizzard raged in the dark outside, the members of the parliament of Canada, by a vote of 91 to 33, agreed to the Quebec Resolutions.

They had come to a great conclusion by a long and anxious road, searching the hopes of the nation in as fine a debate as parliament would ever know. Now it was over and untidily over, as many of history's moments come to their end. 'The House', wrote one irreverent reporter in the gallery, 'was in an unmistakeably seedy condition, having ... eaten the saloon-keeper out, drunk him entirely dry, and got all the fitful naps of sleep that the benches along the passages could be made to yield. Men with the strongest constitutions for parliamentary twaddle were sick of the debate, and the great bulk of the members were scattered about the building with an up-all-night, get-tight-in-the-morning air, impatient for the sound of the division bell. It rang at last at quarter past four, and the jaded representatives of the people swarmed in to discharge the most important duty of all their lives.'

Canada was committed to the cause of Confederation. Its petition would now go forward to the Queen. So much was stirring in the murky loom of the future. But the sky to the east was black and the sky to the south blacker. The Americans threatened while Maritimers gave way, and without union there was small hope of defence. Only London could make this union now, and only London defend it. The mother might still persuade reluctant colonies, the mother might share her strength. It was a clouded hope at five of that snowy morning, and the tired victors knew it as they fought their way to their beds. Drifts sucked at their feet, snow swirled in their faces, and the bell of a distant convent chimed in the wind. They stumbled, exhausted, into their hotels and lodgings and found that sleep came hard.

Yet George Brown had recovered three days later. 'Circumstances have separated us very much in the past year, dear Anne,' he wrote, but now the sacrifices seemed worth while. 'Would you not like that darling little Maggie should be able twenty years hence – when we may be gone – to look back with satisfaction to the share her father had in these great events? For great they are, dearest Anne, and history will tell the tale of them.'

8

The Twilight Months

THE COALITION in Canada had fulfilled its undertaking. As a government pledged to a plan of federal union, it had duly evolved the scheme. It had secured the assent of the province. Now, however, as the great debate in the House gave way to routine business and the session dragged to its close, there were only renewed worries. Problems and pressures mounted but there seemed no way to move. The high partners in government were chafed by the daily harness and uneasy with each other. Brown's distaste for Macdonald was returned with hearty warmth. Galt recovered his old dislike of Brown. Cartier remained for Brown the man of the French, conceded much and not to be conceded more. While the bad news came from the Maritimes, they were hardening in new differences, resurrecting old quarrels. The coalition was straining and the great plan stood still.

There was no hope now for one of the island colonies, and little enough for the other. There was no present hope of securing the return of New Brunswick. Tilley was determined and resourceful but Tilley was out of power, and all his Confederates with him. The project slept in New Brunswick, buried under hostile votes, and it was hardly in better case in Nova Scotia. Tupper, the friend of union, seemed a man besieged and trapped.

As Howe turned against the scheme of union the province had turned with him. The old giant had risen more powerful than ever before, jealous and bitter yet crammed with reasons too. He appealed to the pride and past of the old province, its fear of Canada, its distrust of the French. His gorge rose up at the thought of this thread of peoples, strung out through endless wilderness, calling itself a nation. How could it grow but west, away from the sea, away from England? How could it fail to be swallowed up by the Americans? Howe had dreamed of a great imperial union linked by the sea with England, piercing the west with railways, yet always with London as its heart and source. Where would the heart be now? – in squalid Ottawa. Where were the railways? They were promised again, as many times before, and promises would fail again. Should Nova Scotians turn away from the sea, surrender their powers and pride, taxes and hopes to these promisers, these new-come meddlers of the seventeen days? 'When our people go into mourning, as I believe they will, and wear their flags half-mast on every sea' the 'blunder worse than a crime' would have its answer. 'How long will the system last?' he cried from the stumps. 'Just till the men beside the sea trample it under their feet!'

The sound of the marching feet was already loud. Tupper stood up to it, tough and bold as ever, but he knew that he stood on sand. He had not yet asked his legislature to approve the plan of Quebec; he had not dared to. He was still sure of his delegates and perhaps a dozen others. But the mood of the rest of the House was all too clear. A vote on Confederation would turn him out to the people, and the people stood with Howe. A general election would send him down in ruin, taking the plan with him.

The road ahead for Canada lay confused and thick with obstacles. She had approved the Quebec Resolutions, and her own petition for union was now before the Queen. Yet what could a union mean that did not include at least New Brunswick and Nova Scotia, the two mainland colonies? The hope of the railway and the door on the sea would be gone. There would be the old isolation, the wall of eastern wilderness, and there would be far worse than that; George Brown had made it clear. If the wider confederation should fail, he said, there must still be union for Canada. It must be union not in the old form but in the new, with representation by population conceded, with a parliament sure to be dominated by an Upper Canadian majority. Nothing that Brown had gained could now be lost. That must be a solemn promise, clear and explicit, if he was to remain a member of the coalition. If, by the opening of the session of 1866, this government of which he was a part could not hold out the definite prospect of Confederation, it must propose

the colonies ever more strongly southward.

For the men of the coalition the summer days in England had been a brief, harmonious interlude. They had not much wanted to make the trip together, but it had been necessary and it had been successful. More than that, it had been surrounded by all the colour and brilliance and hospitality with which the great capital wooed its far-off sons. The Canadians had been entertained in the noble mansions and the easygoing country houses, where men who were shaping the greatest affairs of the world talked to them freely and casually. There had been state banquets and state receptions for them. They had mingled with Lords and seen the Lords at play, and had played with them. They had been guests in the Royal Enclosure at Epsom Downs and had come home from the races in the long, riotous procession that always followed. The great in the carriages and the commoners walking by the roadside had laughed and shouted with each other, delivered mock orations, pelted each other by ancient licence and custom with bags of bran and flour and handfuls of peas. Brown and Macdonald, sharing the same carriage and each equipped with a pea-shooter, had traded volleys with the crowd. They had reached their hotel that night like tired boys, rumpled by the fun and dusty-white with flour. They had gone together, in very different garb, to kiss the hand of the Queen. They had been 'The Chambermaid's Delight' that day, as Brown told his Anne, in their full court dress with sword, cocked hat, and knee-breeches.

Now, however, they were back in sober broadcloth. They were back in Canada, with more waiting ahead of them and all the old strains returning. England had given them much of what had been asked. The Colonial Office was firm for Confederation. It had undertaken to persuade the wayward Maritimers and was already busy at the work. But it was not work in which the Canadians could help; their hands were tied. And until the Maritimes moved nothing could move. There were only the rasping cares of daily government, the slowly simmering quarrels and the thought of George Brown's deadline. That promise to Brown hung over the coalition, as near as the next session of the parliament of the provinces of Canada. If Confederation failed, the lesser union must come on Brown's terms.

All through that crowded summer the men of the Maritimes fought their war in London. Tupper and Tilley were there as soon as the Canadians left, asking and getting support. The anti-Confederates followed, by special invitation, loud with their counter-proposals. Howe came as the last of them, the man who must be won. He loved London, he loved Britishness, he loved the glamour of statecraft and the flattery of powerful men. All this the Colonial Office supplied, in generous measure. It reached beyond Howe to plead with the government of New Brunswick and the governments of the island colonies in long and urgent letters. Still, at the end, as all the travellers came home, nothing had moved. Colonial Office injunctions to stubborn colonies had merely served to rouse colonial bristles. Howe was a sterner enemy than before.

It was late autumn before the first glimmerings of hope stirred in New Brunswick. The portly A. J. Smith, Tilley's supplanter, had gone to London as an anti-Confederate and been soberly shaken there. He had come home to find that his hopes for the Western Extension stood bemired. If there was to be no railway linking Saint John with Maine, what of that other link, the promise of Canada? If there was not to be Confederation, what then? The questions were rising now in a confused, distrustful mutter, and they were shaking his hold on the province. How much he did not know, but a straw rose in the wind. Charles Fisher, contesting a by-election in the crucial constituency of York, edged his way to a victory. He was a slippery politician who had been cautiously enigmatic since the fall of Tilley's government. But he was still one of the Confederates, one of the men of Quebec. He had not dared to speak very loud for the plan, yet the votes spoke for themselves. The wind was fitful and inclined to swing.

The election victory was the first good news for Canada in many months, and it came none too soon. The coalition was strident with quarrels now and wearing a new head. Taché had died in August and Sir Narcisse Belleau sat in his place, dividing Scots at war. Another amiable and elderly parliamentarian, quite comfortable in obscurity and reluctant to emerge from it, the new premier had been called to misery in

95

the name of peace. When Taché's chair became vacant Macdonald had edged toward it. Brown had interposed, once more his old grim self. He would not accept Macdonald as head of government. Neither would Macdonald have Brown. Equal they were and equal would remain, if Brown remained at all. Belleau had come as the figurehead with truce, but the truce was nearing its end.

'Thank Providence I am a free man.' On December 19, 1865, the telegram came from her husband to Mrs. George Brown. He had resigned from the coalition; he was rid of the 'scamps' once more. They were all scamps now, all in Macdonald's aura, carrying on in the drab routines of government while union lingered unborn. The routine had chafed Brown and so had the men themselves. He had quarrelled with each in turn while he still held over them all that deadline and that promise. The bitterest final quarrel had been with Galt, circling the weary question of trade with the Americans. Yet behind Galt was Macdonald and beyond Macdonald the fact; George Brown had done his work. He had hacked away the undergrowth, he had blazed a harsh new trail. He saw the road to the narrow land of his promise, and perhaps he saw beyond. But here Brown stopped, and here Macdonald went on.

9

Light in the East

THE CANADIAN coalition had now to prepare itself for the parliamentary session of 1866. Only one thing was certain after the departure of Brown; the opening of that session would be delayed as long as possible. It would be disastrous to report the failure of the Quebec Scheme. It would be equally disastrous to propose a new union of the Canadas on the terms set by Brown. Only a change in the Maritimes could save the situation, and it must be left to the Maritimers to bring the change about. The Canadians, chafed and fretting and overhung by a deadline, must still watch and wait.

The turn of the year brought only competing anxieties. Newfoundland's legislature, opening in January of 1866, speedily dispelled the last lingering hopes for Confederation there. On February 22 Tupper met the Nova Scotia parliament with a Speech From the Throne in which the Quebec Resolutions were not even referred to. 'The government has no policy on

the subject' was the only reply made when confident
anti-Confederates pressed for a statement. The only
present answer to Howe and his gladiators was to
keep the plan from the arena. Worse still, and quite
apart from politics, was the fear of Fenian invasion.
It had now become real both for Canada and the
Maritimes as armed rowdies, discharged from the
Union armies, began to gather and prowl along the
border.

Yet the Fenians, in their own unlikely way, were
contributing to the cause of union. Nor was the gloom
surrounding the plan quite so thick as it had been. In
New Brunswick the anti-Confederate premier, A. J.
Smith, was no Joseph Howe. He had failed in his
railway hopes and he had been damaged in the by-
election campaign that returned Charles Fisher to
parliament. He had evolved no alternative to the
Quebec Scheme and he was being steadily pressed by
London to support the original plan. That he could
not do, but neither could he resist the mood of crisis.
His legislature met on March 8 in a climate of impending war. New Fenian alarms were being sounded
every day. Canada had just called up an additional
ten thousand men of the volunteer militia. The Maritime provinces were crying for mobilization and for
the help of British warships. It seemed to be a time
of danger, calling for common action. Canadians
seemed less alien to New Brunswickers as they
thought of those other aliens below the border. The
wishes of England seemed to carry more weight when
English ships were needed.

As all these pressures crowded in on Smith he felt his support weakening. Unsure of his strength in the House, prodded on by the Governor of New Brunswick who was himself prodded from England, he looked for refuge at last in strategic retreat. He could not endorse the Quebec plan but he could accept the idea of union, some other form of union to be made at some future time. He could admit the views of England while rejecting the terms of Canada. In the Speech From the Throne authorized by the premier the jubilant Governor was 'directed to express to you the strong and deliberate opinion of Her Majesty's Government that it is an object much to be desired that all the British North American colonies should agree to unite in one government'.

The speech proposed no action and neither did Smith. He was very soon to admit that he had no action in mind. But strategic retreat had opened the way to a rout and in three days the reviving forces of union were on the move. On March 12 Charles Fisher leaped to the head of the march with a motion of no confidence. By April 10 the Smith government had resigned and on that same day Tupper went into action in Nova Scotia. The government that had had no policy a month before was now for 'a scheme of union' that would 'effectually ensure just provision for the rights and interests of Nova Scotia'.

It was a move long delayed and very skilfully prepared by another man who had grown. Tupper had gone to the Charlottetown conference as a restless politician. He had left it as a man with the vision of a nation. Quebec had enlarged that vision and nothing had blurred it since. For eighteen months, while Howe stormed through the province and the province rose behind him, Tupper had waited. He had been bland and blank, evasive, persuasive, watchful. He had seen the terms of the Quebec Scheme ripped to shreds, and had seemed to shelve that scheme. But he had kept the idea of union faintly breathing, wafted along even by the wind of Howe. Not even Howe could deny the pulse of the times, the need for change, for growth. His own imperial plannings had foretold it and they still haunted him now. He could mock the terms of Quebec, he could scoff at plans and planners, but he could not point to a better way ahead. He could not deny the hope of a British nation. Nor could he make the crucial men who counted deny it for the sake of Howe.

He stormed at McCully and pleaded with Archibald, the old friends, the pillars of his party in the House. They sat on unmoved. If they could be won over the House would be lost to Tupper, and Confederation with it. Instead, while the cheers outside were a roar for Howe, these two were silent. The bland urgings and ruthless persuasions of Tupper were at work on lesser men. An uneasy premonition stirred in that legislature, growing with the fear of the Fenians and the news that came from New Brunswick. The wind of Howe blew nowhere. Union, some form of union, would have to come. It must be in the end the union made in Quebec, Tupper knew that. He dared not ask for a vote on those seventy-two resolutions; they would only be torn and mangled in new debate. But the key to all was a declaration for union passed by a vote of this House. The odds were chancy still but he reached for the key.

Four nights after Tupper proposed his resolution the Fenians also moved. They had been gathering across the border for more than a week, filling the streets of Portland, Maine, with 'knots and coteries of suspicious looking Americanized Irishmen, carrying revolvers and long dirks in their pants' belts'. Well watched from the Canadian side, and well advertised in the newspapers, they had moved out to Eastport on the Maine coast, just across from New Brunswick. There for a day or two they had held a 'convention', well lubricated by alcohol and inflamed by Celtic eloquence. In the dark of each night they had looked across a narrow stretch of water to Indian Island and Campobello Island, both New Brunswick territory. At midnight on April 14 temptation became too strong and patriotism rose too high in the breasts of five of their number. Crossing in a stolen boat to Indian Island, they held up the customs collector, relieved him of a few dollars, and scuttled back to Eastport with a captured British flag.

The response was swift and a little out of proportion. To some suspicious eyes it seemed over-dramatic. Along the New Brunswick coast, by order of New Brunswick's Governor, five thousand troops and militia were drawn up ready for battle. The British warships *Pylades* and *Niger*, both already on patrol, closed in on Eastport. It was announced that H.M.S.

Tamar and H.M.S. *Simoon* had been summoned from Malta with troops, and on April 17 the flagship H.M.S. *Duncan* with eighty-one guns and most of the Halifax garrison sailed from that port.

The confrontation came at mid afternoon on April 19. While the mighty *Duncan* patrolled the bay off Eastport, towering among her sister ships and filling the sky with smoke, the governors and commanders-in-chief of Nova Scotia and New Brunswick, all in full-dress uniform, went in to meet the Americans. They found, on board the little coastal sloop *Regulator*, General G. G. Meade, the man who had commanded the Union armies at Gettysburg. He was in civilian dress, suffering from a cold in the head, and pleasantly apologetic. He had come up from Philadelphia in his appropriately named vessel to see that there was no more trouble. He had brought a few troops along and the Fenians had decamped at the sight of them, leaving their unpaid board bills. In Eastport the accustomed peace was broken now only by the wails of landlords. The fear of invasion was ended.

The British ships returned to their usual stations and the troops came marching home. It had all been, said angry accusers later, a great show manufactured in support of Confederation. It had not been quite that; the Fenians were real enough and were still to be heard from. But they had been well used here in the delicate work of statecraft. Through a week of debate on Tupper's resolution a heady elixir of danger had filled the air. Ships on the move and troops on the

SIR SAMUEL LEONARD TILLEY

march in Halifax had supported Tupper's reasons. The climax came at two o'clock on the morning of April 18, while crowds in the streets were awaiting the news from Eastport. In the lamp-lit house of the legislature the resolution passed. The power in Nova Scotia, if not the people, had swung to the cause of union.

Tupper was up, Smith was down, but Tilley was still out. New Brunswick, seen from Canada, was now the vital piece in the shifting pattern. Without her, there could be no link between Canada and Nova Scotia, no way to the sea. But New Brunswick, viewed at home, was a clutter of doubts. The going of Smith had lifted up Confederates but it had not solved their problems. They barely controlled the legislature, they were divided among themselves on the form union should take, and their leader without a seat was still looking down from the gallery. There was no power and no will to force a vote in this House. Once more the voice of the province would have to speak.

On May 9 the New Brunswick legislature was dissolved. The Confederates formed round Tilley for the new campaign. In fifteen months, he had said at the time he fell, the people would change their minds. He had now to prove it in as rough a general election as the province would ever know. The polite little one-time druggist seemed the better for his long, enforced rest. There was a new steel in him and a new fire. As the province began to seethe with crowds and banners he discovered a new toughness for the horny-handed business of winning votes. He needed help from Tupper and Tupper responded. He demanded money from Canada and the money was soon in hand, soon spent, and soon replaced. Howe and his Nova Scotians joined the battle; anti-Confederates prayed for Tilley's defeat and paid for the votes to buy it. Everything centred now on this campaign, on this New Brunswick sprawled between Canada and the sea. It lay, the gap in the map, the all-or-nothing of union, while its strident voices echoed from halls and stumps. To beat Tilley was to beat Tupper and Confederation with him, to tear that resolution to useless shreds. On May 25 the balloting began, crawling from poll to poll and town to town. By June 1 enough of the counting was in. Tilley had swept the province and New Brunswick would go for union.

That same day Canada had other news. At dawn on June 1 a thousand Fenians under John O'Neill, an engaging veteran of the Civil War who had become a Colonel at the age of twenty-five, crossed over the Niagara at Fort Erie. They were shabbily dressed in a wide variety of old uniforms and they had the usual Fenian optimism about the thousands of troops who would follow them and the thousands of oppressed Canadians who would give them a welcome. They were, for all that, thoroughly seasoned soldiers and skilful in their trade. Well armed and well disciplined, they moved quietly through a sleeping countryside, only rousing a village with a polite demand for breakfast. They patrolled the streets while the townsfolk hurried to comply, and when the pails of tea and coffee and the great heaps of bread and fried

105

ham were disposed of they slept for a while in the fields, with sentries on watch to prevent damage to the farms and orchards. Then they assembled smartly and moved on, throwing their scouts ahead of them. By dawn of the next day they were deployed along the Ridgeway Road, threatening the Welland Canal and watching Canadian militia debarking at Ridgeway Station.

Four hundred volunteer reserves from Toronto and Hamilton had been rushed to the station under a nervous young colonel who was facing his first action. He did well for a time as his scouts located the enemy and his spread-out line advanced over fields and fences, firing as they came. 'In their red uniforms they presented a beautiful appearance,' O'Neill wrote later, 'one of the prettiest sights I ever witnessed ... the line was well-formed and the advance was brave.'

It was not a very effective advance, as the firing was high and wild and was soon growing ragged for lack of ammunition. O'Neill's veterans, well placed and under cover, would have been well able to deal with it but there were other things to think of. The main body of the Fenians had been depleted by leaving detachments behind along the line of march, and O'Neill was on the watch for other British forces coming up in his rear. He had just decided to draw back toward Fort Erie when bugles sounded in front of him. His men watched incredulously as the British wavered and retired and then formed into the hollow squares that had repelled the Guards of Napoleon at Waterloo. It was quite evident that someone had sounded the wrong call, and the raw youngsters in red were now irresistible targets. The Fenians broke from cover, charged down on the squares and the squares melted away. The pell-mell pursuit went on past Ridgeway Station, only ending as a train puffed gallantly up to take the defeated on board. Stretched on the grass of the fields in the bright morning sunlight lay nine Canadian dead and forty-four wounded.

It was the only battle of the 'invasion'. By nightfall the Fenians, very gingerly prodded by another British force, had edged back to Fort Erie. In the darkness they slipped away across the river, to tell the tale of their exploits for years to come. There were no other thousands to pour across from the United States and reinforce them. There were no slaves of tyrants waiting to rise in Canada. The land was still again.

In that stillness, with those dead and wounded to mourn, the parliament of Canada assembled on June 8 for the first time in Ottawa. It was still the parliament of a province, but the spacious magnificence of the new buildings seemed to promise other things. There was rage at the Fenians, strengthening the wish for union. There was the good news from the Maritimes. There was no longer that hovering fear of George Brown's deadline. His condition had been met; the project of the larger union was clearly in train. There was only the need for haste, always haste; and now it would be Tupper pressing in place of Brown.

10

The Road to London

THE THREADS of the plan were almost drawn together. On June 25 New Brunswick under Tilley confirmed the verdict of the election. The legislature of the province declared itself for union 'upon such terms as will secure the just rights and interests of New Brunswick, accompanied with provision for the immediate construction of the Intercolonial Railway'. There was no endorsement here of the work of Quebec; those dangerous resolutions seemed laid away. In New Brunswick, as in Nova Scotia, they had been too much fought over, too much flayed by criticism and clouded by equivocation to be openly revived now. Yet the common goal had been settled on by four of the six provinces. There remained, in Tupper's view, only the great last step.

Nova Scotia, New Brunswick, and the two Canadas must evolve their final terms, shape them into a Bill and lay that Bill before the Imperial authorities. They must do the work in London, for authority would take a hand. They must do it, mindful of the Imperial parliament which would make the act of union. They must do it also mindful of conditions at home, and here was the crux and key. Once more the calendar governed the fate of the planners. They were faced by another deadline that gave them less than a year.

Time was threatening Tupper now, and threatening the plan with him. In eleven months the term of his government would end. He would be required by law to dissolve his legislature and call a general election. He would have to face the province and face Howe. It would be one thing if he came with a *fait accompli*, as a citizen of a new nation made by a solemn act of the British parliament. He might very well be defeated, and he was quite prepared for that, but the union would not be destroyed. Union would stand and Tupper would rise again; he was sure of that. He was sure of his Nova Scotians when the wind of Howe had passed. He hardly dared to think of the other prospect. He would stand on the stumps with union still unmade, father of that mauled hope, forlorn and tattered, shredded in gales of words. To know the result he had only to look from his windows, walk the streets, read the newspapers. He had only to think of those hundreds of inky scrawls added each day to Howe's monster petitions. Tupper would be out, Howe in, and Confederation a dusty hope for the future. He did not intend to deliver the province to Howe, nor the work of making the nation to unborn men. He intended to get to London and come back, in time, with the work done.

So did Macdonald, in whose hands the threads were gathering. He no longer had Brown to face in the coalition. He was always at ease with Cartier and rarely at odds with Galt. Tupper and Tilley had turned to him from the first as the master politician and the shrewd and resourceful guide. He was in control now, subtly, surely, easily, of the men and minds at work. But he was not in control of events, and events were wayward. Obdurately, entanglingly, through the days of a long, hot summer, they thrust themselves in his path. He walked among them and waited on them, eyeing the dangers ahead. He did not yet wear that nickname, 'Old Tomorrow', but he was beginning to earn it now. Always delaying, hammered at by Tupper, conscious of time as any man, he took his time still.

'We must obtain action during the present session of the Imperial Parliament,' Tupper wrote to him on June 17, 'or all may be lost. Our House expires by law in May next, and for reasons which it is not necessary to enter into here the result would be most disastrous to Confederation.' Macdonald concurred but waited on in Ottawa. Ten days later Tupper himself appeared, hard on the heels of his letter. New Brunswick was now in the fold, Tilley was ready and anxious; it was time to sail for London. Archibald came along with him, equally emphatic. He had pledged his career with Tupper's in the cause of Confederation and was certain to go down with Tupper if it came to a general election. There would be no hope left in either political camp to salvage the cause of union;

there would only be Howe and chaos. There would indeed, said Macdonald, but there was chaos enough here. He would sail when the wind was right.

He hoped that the time might come in late July, and with that hope Tupper returned to Halifax. By July 19 he had waited long enough. So had Tilley. Gathering up their delegates, the two men sailed for London. But they were still to await the Canadians for a long four months.

Macdonald's difficulties had begun with the beginning of the year, on both sides of the Atlantic. He had had to delay the opening of the Canadian parliament until Tupper and Tilley had gained their verdicts for union. Yet that had hardly been done when there was new danger. One day after the passing of Tilley's resolution in New Brunswick, the British government in London fell from power. New men took the helm whose views on Confederation were not yet known. They might be hostile, they might be influenced by the clamour of Howe, and the plan approved by the four provinces might yet be killed in London. Those fears were laid by August. The new British government was as strong for Confederation as the old. It could be approached with confidence. Yet it could not offer the hope of an early decision because it had prorogued parliament. No bill could be submitted and no act passed before the turn of the new year.

There was a perilously close margin for all that remained to be done, and some of the finished work was fraying already. While Howe followed his enemies to London and resumed the battle there, Canada resounded with new conflicts and new fears. They were curiously like the old, some of them, and ominous for the future. George Brown was an enemy again, on every issue but the issue of Confederation. That he supported to the full, rejoicing as much as any man in the gaining of the two Maritime provinces. But he seemed to regard the union as already made, and the last need at an end for even a pretence of harmony. 'John A. was drunk on Friday and Saturday and unable to attend the House. Is it not disgraceful?' The letters came to Anne from Ottawa now, and with a new heat. 'I would as soon think of cutting off my head, as of returning to the government. My whole feelings revolt from having anything to do with such a set.' The outbreak of open war was close at hand.

Worse still, the French of Cartier were newly fretful. He was newly watchful himself. He had followed as closely as any man the long fight in the Maritimes. He had welcomed the resolutions that the two provinces had passed. But they were not the resolutions made in Quebec; they had carefully avoided even the mention of the scheme. He knew how delicately Tupper and Tilley had walked, always cramped by expediencies and taking a step at a time. He admired that balance and skill as a politician but he did not trust the result. This promise of union was not the treaty of peoples, and there could be no union without it.

Amidst the fretting and out of the fretting the question of schools rose, newly unsettled, never to be wholly settled. There were English minorities in

Lower Canada and French minorities in Upper Canada, and they had been granted general safeguards. How far did they extend? What were rights? What were privileges? What was the limit of a concession in practice? The questions affected children, language, religion, the control of parents, and the control of priests. They went to the heart of the pact made in Quebec, they tore at the fraying threads of the coalition. Through bitter, dragging weeks in this last of the old parliaments they threatened the waiting hope of a new and greater one. They were not to be resolved by law, not now. As that grew clear Macdonald moved to postpone them. He had lost Galt in the struggle, the champion of the English minority in Lower Canada. Brown was newly angered, Cartier newly disturbed, and the questions remained unanswered as the session drew to its close. Once more uneasy and once more at odds, with the strains of competing peoples thick in the air, the legislature of the two Canadas died as it had lived.

As autumn came on, the quarrels of parliament were silenced but there were new entreaties from London. Tupper and Tilley, Howe and the anti-Confederates were all there, warring and waiting. The issue was being fought out in public pamphlets, letters to statesmen, talk in the clubs and newspapers, while time passed. Nothing had been gained, nothing was safe, and the loss of all was as near as the next few months. Why did the Canadians delay? Where was Macdonald?

Sometimes an answer came in the Toronto *Globe*.

He was, Brown suggested, with his old friend, the bottle. It was true too often and always part of the truth, for the lonely man went on, sober or drunk, sick or well, finding his own way. He had lost Galt and Galt must be regained, at least for the work in London. The Canadas were shaken and quarrelsome again, Cartier alert and alarmed. They must all be soothed, they must all be reassured. Politics resumed where parliament left off, and there were six weeks more of anxious, aching work.

Then, and at last, it was done. Galt was a friend again, if not a colleague. Cartier was restored as an ally. The Canadas had wavered back to their faith in union, each with its reservations, each resigned. All that remained was to choose the men for London. There would be Cartier and his faithful Langevin. There would be Galt and McDougall and there would be W. P. Howland, a new-comer who had risen in the coalition with the departure of George Brown. Brown himself would be absent and perhaps it was just as well. On November 7 McDougall and Langevin went off. On November 14 while Galt, the man of affairs, was still delayed, Macdonald sailed with the others.

11

The British North America Act

It was tuesday morning, December 4, 1866, when
the six delegates of the Canadas sat down in London
with the five men from New Brunswick and the five
from Nova Scotia. With Tupper there were the familiar figures of W. A. Henry, Adams G. Archibald, and
Jonathan McCully. Peter Mitchell, Charles Fisher,
and John Mercer Johnson had all been with Tilley at
Quebec. But in each of the Maritime delegations, as
in the delegation from Canada, there was one new-
comer reflecting the political upheavals of the past
year. J. W. Ritchie, a Nova Scotia lawyer, had taken
the place of Dickey, and R. D. Wilmot was the new
man from New Brunswick. The meeting-place was a
spacious ground-floor room of the Westminster Palace
Hotel, near to Westminster Abbey and near to the
Houses of Parliament. Here, with those stately re-
minders always at hand, the colonials would work
alone.

They were sixteen in London, where they had been

twenty-three at Charlottetown and thirty-three at Quebec. Fewer men were required because the nub of the problem had been reached; it remained now only to give shape and point to the great decision. Yet there was poignancy as well as purpose in the reduced number. The few were painfully aware of the many who still held off and the many who had turned away. They were shouldering a heavy weight, and the burden was none the lighter for the thought of those absent faces.

It was now two years and three months since that September morning when the first conference had opened. Much had changed in the interval and many of the brightest hopes had gone by the board. Prince Edward Island and Newfoundland had been lost. Nova Scotia had hardly been gained as yet, even though Tupper sat here exuding burly confidence. There were formidable enemies still remaining in New Brunswick, and there was George Brown in Canada who was a friend only to union. For Tupper and Tilley, for Macdonald and Cartier and Galt – all the men who had been the leaders on the long road from Charlottetown – each step of the way had uncovered new dangers and opened onto greater problems. Yet in the end it had brought them to this room. They were no longer visionaries dreaming on a remote island. They had entered the stream of history, of law-giving and nation-making, that had swept William the Conqueror to the hill of Hastings and made the Magna Carta at Runnymede and was still flowing. With the very heart of the empire beating

116

round them, they were here to channel its life and strength and wisdom into the body of a new nation.

They began their work with one central question and one central fear. Upon what basis did their plan stand? Canada had approved the seventy-two resolutions of Quebec. Nova Scotia had not. Neither had New Brunswick. In both Maritime provinces the months of bitter controversy had obscured every issue. They had aroused the fears of federalism, of Canada, of the French. There had been no quieting those fears, no returning to the pact. Tupper and Tilley had won precarious mandates only for union itself, on undefined terms. They were terms to be defined here, in the presence of the imperial mother, and finally with her approval. Were they to be different from the terms of Quebec?

For Macdonald, for Galt, and for most of the English delegates, much might well have been changed. They were still drawn by heart and mind and instinct to the thought of a single people always weaving together under a central head. They still believed that one day that must come, whatever the terms of union. They saw it in the thrust of history, the shape of growth; they saw it written large across the western sky of this continent, already possessed by thirty million English. All this Cartier saw, quite as clearly as they did, knowing their minds and squarely athwart their purpose. He had set his people against the thrust of history, he had challenged facts and time and population, always in the ancient battle for survival. What he had won lay here, intricately embedded in

117

this pact of Quebec, this balanced union and this dual hope/ This he intended to have, or he would have nothing.

It was the rock which had slowly revealed itself during the months of waiting in the Canadas, while Tupper and Tilley fought their Maritime battles. It still held threat of shipwreck for the plan. Yet Macdonald had the helm in his grasp now and he had long since fixed his course. He did not like federalism, he distrusted many of the features in the new plan of government and he hoped one day to change them. But he knew Cartier, as he himself was known, measured him as coolly and trusted him as well. There had been no basis between them but firm and open agreement and there would be no other now. Whatever his hopes of time he left to time. For this day the terms of Quebec must stand./

The winds of discussion stirred a little and stilled, setting Macdonald's way. Tupper and Tilley, those battered realists, had measured their course as he had. They sat alert and aware, in command of their men, shaping their purpose to the shape of the facts. They might have fears and prejudice to confront at home, but those were distant reefs. The rock was here at hand. They faced Cartier with Macdonald beside him. They faced the words of a treaty affirming a dual nation. They were here to appraise, refine, and reaffirm; they were not here to change. And with that the work began.

It went swiftly, for debate was on wording now, not on principle. Within two weeks the resolutions of

SIR JOHN A. MACDONALD

Quebec were nearing their final form as the London Resolutions. By Christmas Eve they were ready. There was a gay holiday pause for tired men, flooded with invitations and welcome in many homes. Then, in the bleak and foggy greyness of a London January, the larger meetings began. Colonials might resolve but the mother would have to decide, and the next step in the nation-making was for the legal counsellors of the state and high colonial officials. They must sit with the delegates, approve the resolutions and ready the work at last for the eyes of parliament. One by one the clauses passed in review, the difficulties rose, and Macdonald manoeuvred round them.

He was watching the hope of Charlottetown and the work of Quebec and London become the language of law, the terms of a Bill. He was parrying now not only familiar fears but the pens of powerful strangers, eager to chop and change. The motherland was well-willed; she was often ill-informed. Her lawyers desired this, her officials suggested that, threatening all too often to reopen an old quarrel. Time after time Macdonald intervened, saving a word, preserving the intent of a clause, while delegates sat beside him frozen and glaring. 'Macdonald,' wrote one of the British counsel afterward, 'was the ruling genius and spokesman . . . the French delegates were keenly on the watch for anything which weakened their securities . . . the Nova Scotia and New Brunswick delegates were very jealous of concessions to the *arrière* province . . . Macdonald had to argue the question with the home government on a point on which the slightest divergence from the narrow line already agreed on in Canada was watched for – here by the French and there by the English – as eager dogs watch a rat hole; a snap on one side might have provoked a snap on the other and put an end to the concord. He stated and argued the case with cool, ready fluency, while at the same time you saw that every word was measured, and that while he was making for a point ahead he was never for a moment unconscious of the rocks among which he had to steer.'

By the first days of February only one rock remained, the question of name and style for the new creation. The four provinces were already designated. They were to be Ontario and Quebec, Nova Scotia and New Brunswick. Canada would comprise the whole, yet what was Canada? A kingdom, Macdonald had said; this should be the Kingdom of Canada. Yet it would be a kingdom all too near to the United States, that raucous hater of kings. The motherland feared to clap that 'monarchical blister' onto the side of a truculent neighbour. Canadians must think again. Their thoughts turned at last to the seventy-second psalm: 'He shall have dominion also from sea to sea'. The new nation, already linked in hope with the western ocean, was to be the Dominion of Canada.

On February 12 the British North America Bill was read for the first time in the House of Lords. On March 8 the British North America Act emerged from the House of Commons, passed on its third reading. To delegates, who watched from the galleries after their months and years of work, this last great stage had seemed a deflating process. 'They want to get rid of us,' said a resentful Galt. There had been many empty seats on the floor of the Commons; there had been little eloquence and no fire. A few British members had echoed the complaints of Howe, a few others had refuted them, but most had seemed indifferent to the fate of the far-off colonies. Yet this was still parliament, reflecting and directing history with its sleepy rumble of 'ayes'. Out of the dull debates had emerged a hail-and-farewell worthy of the mighty mother.

'In geographical area,' said the Earl of Carnarvon, the Colonial Secretary, 'this Confederation of the British North American Provinces . . . may become one day second only in extent to the vast territories of Russia . . . in population, in revenue, in trade, in shipping, it is superior to the Thirteen Colonies when, not a century ago, in the Declaration of Independence, they became the United States of America. We are laying the foundations of a great state – perhaps one which at a future date may even overshadow this country. But, come what may, we shall rejoice that we have shown neither indifference to their wishes nor jealousy of their aspirations, but that we honestly and sincerely, to the utmost of our power and knowledge, fostered their growth, recognizing in it the conditions of our own greatness.'

The delegates prepared for home. There were wide and thrilling horizons now but the clouds still hung thick. There were the problems of fitting together the machinery of union, and there was the greater problem of a mutinous Nova Scotia. The railway was still to be built, that promised link with the sea. The thought of the great west crowded in on them and could not be thrust aside. They were returning, English and French, joined in faith and confidence, yet knowing their separate minds. Among the competing hopes no man could judge, no man decide. Only time could realize, only time could reconcile; it would still be men unborn who would crown the work.

Macdonald came home with the largest share of the honours and the heaviest of the burdens. He would be the first Prime Minister of the new Dominion; that was already certain. He had taken over the work begun in spite of him and had made it his own. He would live with it now to the end, growing with it, shaping it, and shaped by it. Nor would he be the same now, even as a private man. He had found at fifty-two, in spite of the cares and hopes and quarrels of statecraft, that statesmen could fall in love.

Agnes Bernard was the sister of Hewitt Bernard, Macdonald's secretary, who had been secretary to the Quebec conference and also the London conference. Macdonald had known her slightly when she lived for a while in Canada, and then had forgotten her when she moved with her mother to London. He had met her again on a casual walk in Bond Street and stopped for a chat that had grown to many others. She was with him now in Canada, the bride of less than a month, who was soon to be first lady. Everything would be different for Macdonald now, the country, politics, and life itself. He would often find the height he had climbed to lonely but he would not be a man alone.

12

The Dominion of Canada

On March 29, 1867 the Queen gave royal assent to the British North America Act and established July 1 as the date for its proclamation. One day later the government of the United States completed a bargain with Russia by which it acquired Alaska. The long retreat of old-world power continued; the North Americans now were nearly alone.

They were still divided under the two flags, and each of the flags was in motion. It seemed a race that could only quicken, always to its old accompaniment of threats and complaints and fears. The Confederation-to-be would endanger Maine, or so said Maine's governor. Americans, said a British Columbian, had only purchased Alaska to sandwich British Columbia, and now could eat her up. Even to Galt, that cool, long-headed man, the facts of the map seemed clear. 'If the United States desire to outflank us on the west, we must . . . lay our hands on British Columbia and the Pacific Ocean. This country cannot be surrounded by the United States – we are gone if we allow it.'

He spoke within five weeks of his return from London, and the words seemed very big. The Dominion of Canada was unproclaimed, the Intercolonial Railway was unbuilt, and his larger hopes were not even projects on paper. The iron realities were the Laurentian Shield, the wild Territories, the empty prairies and the mountains and forests beyond them. This was the way to the west, but how to take it? The difficulties were hardly to be thought of by this narrow ribbon of nationhood that would lie stretched out from the Atlantic to the Great Lakes. Even within its boundaries the problems of wilderness and distance were still to be surmounted. There were still poverty and isolation and weakness. There was still discord, flaring once more its old, unbanished self.

There would be no reconciliation between Macdonald and Brown. That hope, if hope it had been, was clearly gone. Those two would resume their war in the new nation. Cartier was newly assailed in the province he had made Quebec; Tilley had found his beaten enemies refreshed. Yet none of these, nor all of them together, equalled the threat of Howe in Nova Scotia.

'We have been entrapped into a revolution,' he was crying to the province now. 'You look into each other's faces and ask, "What is to come next?" You grasp each other's hands as though in the presence of sudden danger. You are a self-governed and independent community no longer. The institutions founded by your fathers, and strengthened and confirmed by your

own exertions, have been overthrown. Your revenues
are to be swept beyond your control. You are hence-
forward to be governed by strangers, and your hearts
are wrung by the reflection that this has been done
not by the strong hand of open violence but by the
treachery and connivance of those whom you trusted,
and by whom you have been betrayed.' Tupper was
the trusted man battered by those assaults. He was
undismayed, he had expected them and prepared for
them, and he had won his race with time. Buttressed
now by an Act of the British Parliament, he would
deliver Nova Scotia into the union. Yet what could
it be there but the ticking bomb, certain to explode
and bring the union down? How could the flimsy
fabric stand secure, faced by that prospect? How
could it rise at all?

No man quite knew and yet it somehow rose,
powerless and lifeless, but a portent still. Through the
late spring the old legislatures of the Maritime pro-
inces-to-be lived out their twilight lives and brought
them to a close. The framework of new legislatures
and the framework of central government took shadowy form. There was a sense of deeper, weightier
change throbbing beneath the surface of everyday.

Nothing would be the same now. It was as true for
the old colonies who had rejected union as for those
whom union would embrace. The two islands still
apart in the Atlantic could not but feel the power of
new forces, the tug of new interests, drawing them
westward up the length of the river. Already the
Maritime mainland thought with Canada, often de-

ploring, fearing and resisting change, yet concerned by the same concerns. A tide of acquiescence began to set, sullenly and slowly, even in Nova Scotia, even in Howe. He would not admit it, he would still fight on to the end, for change, for vengeance on the men who had won. 'We have to mourn the loss of our independence, to fit a strange yoke upon our necks . . . to look at a future full of peril and uncertainty.' Yet as he studied that future, not to be avoided now, the eloquent forebodings weakened. 'A year hence, or five years hence, we may . . . have cause to rejoice . . . There may come a time when the 1st of July may be a day of cheerfulness in Nova Scotia.'

There were other foreshadowings as the 1st of July drew near. Beyond Dominion Day lay the great problem of the west, not to be avoided or postponed. The Territories must be taken into the union. They could not be left in the hands of the Hudson's Bay Company, a preserve of trapper and trader, where the buffalo or the beaver was more welcome than the settler. If Canadian sovereignty did not reach out to embrace that vast, empty region, then American sovereignty would. 'I would be quite willing, personally,' John A. Macdonald had said two years before, 'to leave that whole country a wilderness for the next half century.' But there was no leaving it; there could be no waiting. There must soon be an answer also to the cry from the farther west, 'that . . . His Excellency take such steps without delay as may be deemed by him most desirable to ensure the admission of British Columbia into the Confederacy on fair and equal terms.' The hope born in Charlottetown, and rejected now in Charlottetown, had become a command and promise reaching to the other ocean.

Steadily the bones of the nation came together, to walk when the flesh came, when the spark of life was given. The frameworks of the local legislatures and of the central parliament were set up, to await their filling at a general election. That could not come until the nation was made, and it was sure to be a stormy coming. There would be George Brown, the party leader again, eager to turn Macdonald out of his place. There would be Howe in Nova Scotia, powerful still, and still chafed and revengeful. There would be many wars but all within the walls of the union and the union would stand now; Macdonald was sure of that. He could deal with Brown; he was sure of that too. He was not so sure, for many a long week, that he could solve the central, crucial riddle of government.

That was the making of the cabinet. It was to be the nightmare of all men who would stand thereafter in his place. Rising out of parliament, under the Prime Minister, the cabinet must rule the nation. It must reflect the image of the nation; it must represent in proportion Protestants and Catholics, English and French, and it must not forget the many thousands of Irish. The great and varied interests, the sources of life and growth must each be spoken for; the trade that looked to the sea, the inland trade, forestry and factories, ships and shops, commerce and farms. They were all authentic parts of the common pattern; they all interlocked and yet they all competed. Each would speak for itself, they would all contend in the cabinet, and they must all be held in balance to guide the nation. Clamorous and tugging, intricate as life itself, here was the essence and the core of power.

Yet cabinets were made of men, hungry for power. The men must be chosen now, and chosen by Macdonald. They would be the first rulers of the new Dominion, subject to elections when elections came but until then supreme. Each must speak for a segment of the nation's pattern. They should be the best of the spokesmen to be found. They should all be chosen from among the deserving, those seasoned veterans of the work of union. Yet how to make them truly the sum of the work? Which of those men could measure his own worth, his own weight? There were many now like Jean-Charles Chapais, brooding while Macdonald pondered; remembering the work done, the risks taken, thinking of the prizes ahead. 'What will there be for me from these arrangements?' that Father of Confederation had asked his wife. 'Truly I know nothing of it . . . John A. finds me a good fellow – Cartier – that's an enigma! He knows I haven't much ability, but does he know the number of my friends and the moral force I bring to the government? I think not.' Few were as mildly resigned as Jean-Charles Chapais, and few indeed would include the modest injunction. 'Pray for me. I have need of help from on high, for I am not very clever by myself.'

The cabinet-making went on, cautiously and secretly, while urgent politicians competed with urgent forces. Balancing the forces, how to balance men?

Balancing the demands of men, what of the forces?
One by one the men settled into their places, deserving, delicately balanced, complained-of, envied.
Cartier and Galt, Tilley, McDougall, Archibald,
Howland and Mitchell, Campbell and Langevin were
all included. Chapais's speculations came to a happy
conclusion; he found his seat. There remained one
place and there remained two men – Tupper, the
indispensable, and McGee, the prophet of union. If
the one came in the other must remain out. Yet either
man in alone would unbalance the cabinet. McGee
meant too much weight for the Catholic Irish of
Quebec, Tupper too much for Maritime Protestants.
That was how the riddle read in Macdonald's eyes;
that way the threads had pulled.

It was Tupper who cut the knot with one brisk
stroke. He knew his worth and knew the price he
could ask. He meant to have it, but not yet awhile.
Tupper could wait. He had Howe to deal with yet in
Nova Scotia. He would come to the cabinet, when he
came at last, dragging that battered captive in his
train. McGee had hopes as high and less of patience,
but there was the strain of greatness in him too. He
stood aside with Tupper and a lesser man came in.
The cabinet was made.

The June days lingered by and the last day came.
It was almost gone, almost the stroke of midnight on
a stifling Sunday in Toronto, when George Brown
came into the office of the *Globe*. The presses were
waiting for the Monday editorial. He would not write
it on the Sabbath but he was here to write it now. His

pages for months past had thundered against Macdonald. He looked forward to the coming battle of the elections, to throwing that man from power, to unseating that cabinet in which he had found no place, wanted no place. He wished to take hold himself of this nation he had helped to make, and guide its course. He never would, and perhaps in his heart he knew it. 'I am a governmental impossibility,' he had said, and he had not forgotten the words. It was better, he was to say years later, 'that I should not be in the first Parliament of the Dominion, so that old feuds might die out, and the contests of public life be freed from . . . bitterness.' There was to be no power and little honour for George Brown in the new Dominion, and yet there was enough already for pride and peace. The Dominion was almost here, a body to be quickened to life in a few hours.

He took a vast gulp of water from the pail in his office, called for pens and paper and began to write, while the copy boy lurked outside and the printers waited by their presses. It was to be a long night for all of them. 'We hail the birthday of a new nationality,' he wrote as his first words. 'A United British America, with its four millions of people, takes its place this day among the nations of the world.' The pen flowed more quickly, page after page was tossed aside to the boy to be rushed along to the type-setters, as the man who had begun so much on that far-off May morning in the Legislative Building at Quebec retraced the course of the work.

It had grown out of him and of men before him and

131

Hon. George Brown

of men about him. It had broken many of their moulds, defeated many of their purposes, and would defeat many more. It was beyond them now, greater than each, greater than all together, a life to be soon in motion of itself. Yet it must live and thrive by what they had given, the slender little that was all they had; hope, rooted in good will. From those high moments, now already gone, that must endure. The two peoples had come together in hope. The vast distances were bridged by hope, the scattered colonies were joined by hope, deferred, denied, unrecognized by some. Yet with good will that hope was irresistible, never to be stayed again. The man in the office felt it, rose with the hope. He wrote once more in the mood of the high, lost moments, traversing the continent with his hurrying pen, drawing the peoples together, thrusting them on. The darkness at the windows lightened and he was still writing. There was a stir in the streets outside, a first wakening of the ripple of celebration. It would run from city to city and town to town, wavering, fitful and disputed yet, dwarfed by the mighty background of space and forest. Dawn came and he was still writing; it was daylight and growing warm. A murmur of voices came from the courtyard below. There were people waiting at the door of the *Globe*, wanting their Monday paper, wondering at the delay.

Then he was done. The copy boy dashed out of the office with the last sheets. There was a clack of machines, a gathering rumble of presses, and George Brown rose from his desk in the broad sunlight of Dominion Day. He took a last gulp of water from the pail on the floor and struggled into his coat. Then he went home to sleep. He would sleep the day through.

Outside in the courtyard the wet sheets came at last to the waiting people. They reached for them eagerly, hungry for George Brown's words, as they had been for most of their lives. They read the salutation. They followed the vast discourse in its voyage over the continent, its voyage through time and history. They came to the sum of promise, the core of hope: 'that the people who now or hereafter shall inhabit the Dominion of Canada...who shall populate the northern half of the continent from the Atlantic to the Pacific, shall, under a wise and just government reap the fruits of well-directed enterprise, honest industry and religious principle...in the blessings of health, happiness, peace, and prosperity. SO MOTE IT BE.'

In Ottawa a few hours later, while the troops marched and formed on Parliament Hill, the men came together who were to begin the fulfilment of the hope. They walked soberly up the stone steps and along the echoing corridors to confront the Governor General. They took their oaths, received their commissions of office in the name of the Sovereign, and the great stream flowing by Hastings on from Runnymede passed into the body of their nation and made it live. They came out, charged with the hopes and burdens, and the day passed. Celebrations died out, the last rocket flickered across the sky and the sky darkened. Only the buildings on the hill by the river, still too great for the little town about them, stood outlined in light.

CONFEDERATION DAY.

lakes, and destined ere long to embrace the larger half of this North American continent from the Atlantic to the Pacific.

The D

HIST

HOW
BEE

STATIST

Extent
and

y acknowledge the
oser of E
t, pregn
on the co.
bitants of
eming millie
ill people the
cean to ocean,
the annals of
, too, the sa-
forgetfulness
siderations, on
o which under
ception of the
an Confedera-
o a successful
ient labour, a
al concessions,
ed willingness
interests to
would be
f the whole
the result we
ver have been
t three years
y an unreason-
work of such
Mr. Brown,
ugall, as repre-
Upper Canada,
acdonald, Mr.
associates,
whose single and
be to aim at the
Provinces of a new
nce, in which we
peculiar evils and
itherto obstructed
on a happier and
Government was
ne, 1864. On the
ess the fruition of
aken. The public
Provinces joined in

With t
midsumm
of a new
America,
takes its
of the w
name, which
record sufficien
to be perpetu
hensive impor
CANADA, on
in the year of
and sixty-seve
of national ex
passed away.
with its contra
divisions of U
West, has been
new volume is opened, New Brunswick
and Nova Scotia uniting with Ontario
and Quebec to make the history of a
greater Canada, already extending from
the ocean to the head waters of the great

the good work, the sympathy and support of the great mass of the people were soon found to be heartily enlisted in the movement, the cordial and generous co-operation of the mother country was given to